Yale Studies on White-

Crimes of the Middle Classes

White-Collar Offenders
in the Federal Courts

David Weisburd, Stanton Wheeler,
Elin Waring, and Nancy Bode

Yale University Press

New Haven and London

Published with assistance from the foundation established in memory of William McKean Brown.

Designed by James J. Johnson.
Set in Century Schoolbook type by Keystone Typesetting Company, Orwigsburg, Pennsylvania.
Printed in the United States of America by BookCrafters, Inc., Chelsea, Michigan.

Library of Congress Cataloging-in-Publication Data
Crimes of the middle classes : white-collar offenders in the federal courts / David Weisburd . . . [et al.].
   p. cm. — (Yale studies on white-collar crime)
Includes index.
ISBN 0-300-04952-8 (cloth)
      0-300-05946-9 (pbk.)
   1. White-collar crimes—United States. I. Weisburd, David.
II. Series.
KF9350.C75   1991
345.73′0268—dc20
[347.305268]   90-20073
                                              CIP

The paper in this book meets the guidelines for permanence and durability of the Committee on Production Guidelines for Book Longevity of the Council on Library Resources.

10 9 8 7 6 5 4 3 2

To my parents and to Shelly, Sarit, Ariel, and Noam (D.W.)

To my mentor Clarence Schrag and to my sons, Steven, Kenneth, and Warren—great teachers all (S.W.)

To Tommy (E.W.)

To Verna (N.B.)

Contents

Figures and Tables

Preface

This book reports the results of the fourth and final study conducted under a grant from the National Institute of Justice to Yale University and published by Yale University Press in a series entitled Yale Studies on White-Collar Crime. As director of the research program, I want to acknowledge at the outset our indebtedness to the National Institute and their foresight in being willing to provide generous funding for a broad program of research, the precise details of which could only be dimly perceived when the program was launched. This required a degree of institutional trust on their part that is often lacking in relationships between sponsors and researchers. The resulting freedom enabled us to design projects in areas where we could obtain special access to new bodies of data and to take advantage of the special talents and skills of individual researchers.

We made a decision early on to focus on the control of white-collar crime rather than on causation—to focus more on regulatory and law enforcement and on the judicial process than on the situations of the white-collar offenders themselves. This resulted in part from our original commitment to study the sentencing of white-collar offenders. Also, we had a sense that the whole process of criminal justice as it operates in connection with white-collar crime was different than for common crime, and we needed to document that process in detail.

Finally, this focus was one that could take maximum advantage of our institutional location in a major law school.

The three volumes preceding this one reflect these choices. In the volume that initiated this series, Susan Shapiro's *Wayward Capitalists,* we have the first detailed examination of how the Securities and Exchange Commission (SEC) works. It is an extended exploration of the theme that where you look for illegality determines what you will find: how the SEC's intelligence apparatus is organized determines the kinds of violators it catches. In the second volume, Kenneth Mann's *Defending White-Collar Crime,* we are given an in-depth ethnographic account of how lawyers use legal rules and arguments on behalf of their clients, and especially of how important to white-collar-crime defense work is "information control"—how the attorney shapes and constrains the very pool of facts that becomes the basis for legal evidence and argument. In the third volume, Wheeler, Mann, and Sarat's *Sitting in Judgment,* the authors show through interviews with federal judges how they draw upon a common body of social and legal norms—a kind of informal common law—to arrive at their sentences in white-collar-crime cases.

This final volume is in one important respect a departure from the concentration on control and the behavior of officials. Although in its latter chapters we explore the movement of white-collar defendants through the legal system and examine their fate at the time of sentencing, the bulk of the book's early chapters is devoted to the offenders themselves, their backgrounds and offenses, and the relation between the two: how personal situations and organizational opportunities combine to enable some offenders to do much greater damage in the number, magnitude, and duration of offenses than do others.

That we were able to explore these matters in depth and detail is due largely to our good fortune in obtaining access to the presentence investigation reports compiled for convicted federal offenders by federal probation officers. These reports provide a depth of background detail on both the offender and the offense that is simply unavailable from other sources. They are rarely accessible to the research community, but in this case a congressional interest in the sentencing of white-collar offenders led to a special agreement between the Federal Probation Office and Yale that provided for confidentiality of all personal data while allowing the records to be examined for research purposes. We are greatly indebted to Don Chamlee, Chief of the Division of Probation, U.S. Courts, for his help and cooperation in this enterprise.

We believe that this study makes a fundamental contribution to our understanding of the nature of white-collar crime, and to a reformulation of that understanding. But interpretation of the results of any empirical inquiry is necessarily constrained by the precise nature of the cases studied and the data gathered on those cases. Most of these concerns, particularly the nature of the crimes singled out for treatment as "white collar" and the problems of sample selection bias that stem from studying only convicted offenders, are discussed fully in the text. There is one question, however, that has arisen in many discussions of our project with others, and I would like to address it here. This is the question of whether our findings, gathered from a sample of offenders convicted or sentenced in fiscal years 1976–78, would still be true as we enter the decade of the 1990s. No matter how valid they may be for their time, what is their relevance in today's world of criminal justice?

The answer is not a simple one and is different for different parts of our inquiry. Changes in prosecution policy during the Reagan administration would yield more cases of insider trading today and would alter to some degree the nature of offender backgrounds, as well as offenses. We have no Ivan Boesky or Dennis Levine, for example. Empirical studies will always be "out of date" in the narrow sense that current policies will virtually always be different in detail from past practices. Sometimes those differences will be relatively invisible. At other times, when they capture the fancy of the media, as in the insider-trading cases, they will become widely known. In such cases they alter the visible shape of the tip of the iceberg, but there is no reason to believe they alter the nature of the underlying processes.

In our study, for example, we see no reason to believe that the role of organizational opportunity in white-collar crime, as described in chapter 4, is any different in substance in 1990 than it was in the late 1970s, although the particular organizations singled out for public inquiry and prosecution may well have changed. Foreign corrupt practices were the target of the mid 1970s, insider trading and military contracting those of the late 1980s.

Over long stretches of time there are undoubtedly changes in the distribution of types of criminal activity that are great enough to amount to a serious change in the nature of the crime problem. In this century the shift in the locus of economic activity from individual entrepreneurs to corporate enterprise is one such change. It is no accident that a central theme in our analysis is the manipulation of organizational resources for personal gain. But these are shifts seen over decades of societal change, and they in no way invalidate the kinds of generalizations suggested in the early part of our book.

It is a different matter when we consider the movement of offenders through the legal system, as in chapter 5, or the sentencing of offenders, as in chapter 6. Here changes in policy may act directly on the offender population to change the nature of the underlying relationship. We show in chapter 5, for example, that in the late 1970s it was the minor player in an organized scheme who was more often recorded as having cooperated with government investigators. If cases become big enough and complex enough, the government may find that it takes a central insider's cooperation to nail several other defendants. If prosecutors give breaks to central organizers of schemes with any frequency, the underlying relationship will change. In this case "He or she who profited least from the crime will gain the most from cooperating with the government" would be changed to "He or she who gained the most from the crime will also gain the most from cooperating with the government." This description seems to fit the Ivan Boesky case.

Our findings regarding sentencing of white-collar offenders may or may not be valid for the 1990s, depending on the final outcome of some controversial issues facing the U.S. Sentencing Commission. Our chapter 6 records the factors that federal judges were apparently taking into account when they had broad discretion in sentencing. The Federal Sentencing Act of 1984 and the resulting guidelines adopted in 1987 greatly limit that discretion. They require that some factors the judges are already taking into account, like the dollar magnitude of the offense and the prior criminal record of the offender, be formally recognized in every case. But they also mandate that some factors the judges were considering, like the defendant's moral character as judged from his prior life history apart from crime, be systematically excluded from consideration. Whether or not this happens in fact will depend both on the final policies adopted by the Sentencing Commission and on whether judges will find subtle ways to bring in those considerations that they think should count, despite the strictures of the sentencing guidelines. If judges do abide by the guidelines currently in place, some of the underlying relationships that are discussed in chapter 6 will be strengthened, and others will disappear.

This is a long answer to a seemingly short and simple question, but, I hope, one that does the question justice. The short answer is that generalizations about the nature of white-collar criminality are probably as true now as then, but that generalizations that immediately implicate the behavior of public officials like prosecutors and judges may be subject to change.

Some coauthored works are essentially a putting together of individual contributions but this was a genuine collaboration. Nancy Bode was centrally involved in the data collection and early analysis phase when she was also a Yale law student, but not in the later stages of the project, when her duties in the attorney general's office for the State of Minnesota (prosecuting, among others, white-collar offenders) precluded her heavy involvement. Elin Waring was centrally involved in the latter phases, during all aspects of the final analysis and writing, though she bears no responsibility for the original project design. David Weisburd has been involved from inception to completion, at every stage of design and analysis. The book would not have been completed without him. Although our individual voices are heard here and there throughout the manuscript, the writing has been a collective effort.

We are indebted to a number of people for their contributions to the project. In roughly chronological order they include Winifred Reed, who monitored the program for the Department of Justice, James A. McCafferty of the Administrative Office of the United States Courts, who provided the necessary data for sample selection, the aforementioned Don Chamlee, whose office provided the presentence reports, Diana Polise-Garra, who supervised the coding procedures, Robert Gandossy and Mitchell Rothman, who wrote the first substantive memoranda about the nature of the offenders and offenses, and Susan Shapiro and Kenneth Mann, authors of other volumes in the white-collar-crime series, who also read the manuscript and offered comments through the various stages, and my secretary, Gayle Van Dole, for a variety of important services. The support of the broader Yale community has been acknowledged in detail elsewhere but deserves repetition here.

The manuscript was read in whole or in part by a number of colleagues in the field, and we are much in their debt: John Braithewaite, Dan Freed, Lawrence M. Friedman, Abraham S. Goldstein, John Hagan, John Laub, Leon Lipson, Michael Levi, Andrew von Hirsch, and Kate Stith. Gilbert Geis not only gave it a critical reading but also lent it his practiced, journalistic editorial eye, as did Marcia Chambers. We also wish to acknowledge a special indebtedness to one another for putting project ahead of self at critical times when, as all who have done collaborative work know, it might have been the other way around.

Finally, I want to express my own appreciation to the entire staff of Yale University Press for their help in bringing the written products of a major research program to an audience larger than the sometimes insular research community that produces such work.

Stanton Wheeler

Crimes of the Middle Classes

1

Introduction

The commission of wrongs through fraud is as old as human society. Although the concept of white-collar crime did not come into use until the noted criminologist Edwin H. Sutherland coined it some fifty years ago,[1] sociologists in the early twentieth century recognized a type of criminal who "picks pockets with a railway rebate, . . . cheats with a company prospectus instead of a deck of cards, or scuttles his town instead of his ship."[2] Thus, Americans' current attention to forms of white-collar crime represents a return to long-standing problems and issues.

For scholars, concern with white-collar crime has provided an

1. Sutherland first used the term during his presidential address to the American Sociological Society in December 1939. The address was published as "White-Collar Criminality," *American Sociological Review* 5, no. 1 (February 1940):1–12.

2. E. A. Ross, *Sin and Society: An Analysis of Latter-Day Iniquity* (Boston: Houghton Mifflin, 1907). John Braithwaite ("White Collar Crime," *Annual Review of Sociology* 11 [1985]:1–25) notes that Ross was not alone in this early concern with white-collar crime. See Wilhelm A. Bonger, *Criminality and Economic Conditions* (Boston: Little, Brown, 1916); Ida M. Tarbell, *The History of the Standard Oil Company* (New York: Macmillan, 1904); Lincoln Steffens, *The Shame of the Cities* (New York: Doubleday, Page, 1903); and Upton Sinclair, *The Jungle* (New York: Doubleday, Page, 1906).

important contrast, some might say, balance, to the overwhelming preoccupation of researchers with the crimes of poorer Americans. White-collar crime is for most scholars "upper world" or "upper class" criminality.[3] It represents an opportunity both to explore and to challenge theories about crime and deviance in a context that has little in common with that ordinarily associated with criminality. Whether used to support such theories or to challenge them, the concept of white-collar crime has played an important role in the development of criminological theory.[4] As Donald Newman noted some thirty years ago: "The concept of white-collar crime has forced the theoretician into an analysis of highly complex and very abstract relationships within our social system. No longer is the criminologist a middle-class observer studying lower-class behavior. He now looks upward at the most powerful and prestigeful strata, and his ingenuity in research and theory will be tested, indeed!"[5]

In many ways the opportunities that criminologists recognize in examination of white-collar crime and the public's concerns with these questions develop from similar assumptions. For ordinary Americans, prosecution of white-collar crime represents a balancing of the scales of justice. White-collar crime evokes images of rich and powerful Americans often immune from apprehension and prosecution in the criminal justice system, Americans who can use their power in ways that lead them to be rewarded rather than punished for their misdeeds.[6] Just as for scholars the problem of white-collar crime allows a balancing of views of the criminal world by providing a

3. See, for example, Donald Newman, "White-Collar Crime," *Law & Contemporary Problems* 23 (1958):735–53; Herbert Edelhertz, "White Collar and Professional Crime: The Challenge for the 1980s," *American Behavioral Scientist* 27 (1983):109–28; and James Coleman, *The Criminal Elite* (New York: St. Martins, 1989).

4. Sutherland himself used white-collar crime to challenge conventional theories linking crime to poverty and social disorganization, at the same time that he saw the concept as supporting his own theory of differential association. Edwin H. Sutherland, *White Collar Crime: The Uncut Version* (New Haven: Yale University Press, 1983), 260–64. For a more recent example of this same approach, see Travis Hirschi and Michael Gottfredson, "Causes of White Collar Crime," *Criminology* 25 (1987):949–74.

5. Newman, "White-Collar Crime," 753.

6. See, for example, Jeffrey H. Reiman, *The Rich Get Richer and the Poor Get Prison: Ideology, Class and Criminal Justice* (New York: John Wiley & Sons, 1979).

view up as well as down the class ladder, for ordinary Americans it offers a slightly different type of balance—placing them between the criminality of the rich and the criminality of the poor.

In the following chapters we examine these images of white-collar crimes and criminals in the context of a large empirical study of white-collar offenders prosecuted in the federal court system. Contrary to the portrait of white-collar crime generally presented by scholars and in the press, we find a world of offending and offenders that is very close to the everyday lives of typical Americans. Some of those we examine are indeed located far above middle-class status and use resources to commit their crimes and avoid punishment that are unavailable to all but the most privileged. And indeed these criminals are as alien to middle-class citizens as are the poor who are popularly associated with most street crimes. But the majority occupy positions in society that are neither far above nor far below the middle, and their crimes do not necessitate, nor do their defenses rely upon, elite social status. Opportunities to commit these crimes are available to average Americans.

When Edwin H. Sutherland coined the term *white-collar crime,* he gave voice to an interest that has been pursued more in political and rhetorical terms than through sustained empirical examination. We attempt here to extend the empirical tradition by examining closely those who are convicted of white-collar crimes, the offenses they commit, and their experiences as they move through the legal system. We believe that ours is a broader portrait of white-collar crime and its punishment than that developed in prior research, and our findings yield a number of insights into the world of white-collar crime that contradict common assumptions. But we recognize that the nature of what we learn is strongly linked to the strategy we used in developing our study. As a result, we must begin with a brief review of the history of the study of white-collar crime and its role in determining how we chose offenders to be included in our analyses.

White-Collar Crime: History of an Idea

White-collar crime is a social rather than a legal concept, one invented not by lawyers but by social scientists.[7] It has served in

7. This is in contrast, for example, to homicide, for which both commenta-

many ways more as a moral idea than a scientific abstraction. Indeed from the outset the concept of white-collar crime has been used by social scientists and others to extend the stigma of criminality beyond immigrants and the poor to those who occupy positions of power and trust in American society. The idea that the advantaged, like the disadvantaged, may be prone to criminality, but that their crimes are of a different type, fit easily into the American tradition of reform. For criminologists it also provided an avenue of inquiry that challenged common assumptions about the root causes of criminal behavior.

Sutherland addressed both the moral and theoretical problems that white-collar criminality raises. He was scathing in his criticism of the legal system's apparent disregard for the serious harm that white-collar crimes caused.[8] His observation that white-collar crimes resulted in many times the monetary loss of more common criminal offenses provided clear evidence of the seriousness of white-collar criminal conduct. His discussion of the ways in which white-collar offenders avoided criminal prosecutions and their stigma illustrated the differential treatment of low- and high-status offenders in the criminal justice system. Overall, as Colin Goff has observed, Sutherland himself appeared to be full of moral indignation when writing about white-collar crime, indignation that was not evident in his other work.[9]

Whatever Sutherland's moral concerns, his major focus was upon the challenge that white-collar crimes presented to the dominant criminological theories of his day. Most scholars and laypersons then, as today, stressed poverty and social disorganization when developing explanations for criminality. The dominant themes were best stated by urban sociologists at the University of Chicago who believed that economic deprivation, ethnic heterogeneity, and high rates of mobility associated with the poorer areas of America's inner

---

tors and codes go to great pains to establish clear definitions and distinctions between types of crimes and the states of mind of the individuals who commit them. See Stanton Wheeler, "White Collar Crime: History of an Idea," *Encyclopedia of Crime* (New York: Free Press, 1983), 1652–56; Gilbert Geis, "From Deuteronomy to Deniability: A Historical Perlustration on White Collar Crime," *Justice Quarterly* 5 (1988):7–32.

8. Sutherland, *White Collar Crime.*

9. See Colin Hartford Goff, "Edwin H. Sutherland and White Collar Crime." Ph.D. diss., University of California, Irvine, 1983, especially 31.

cities were the primary causes of crime.[10] Sutherland aimed to weaken such theories, while providing support for his own social-learning approach to crime causation—the theory of differential association.[11] Obviously, perspectives that spoke of poverty and social disorganization were inadequate to explain the criminality of high-status business and professional people. His views, which looked to the associations that foster criminality and the normative framework that defends it, were easily transferred to white-collar crime.

Perhaps because of Sutherland's dual moral and theoretical concerns, he was casual in his conceptualization of white-collar crime. At various times he stressed crimes committed by individuals of high social status, crimes carried out in the course of an occupation, or crimes committed by organizations or by individuals acting in organizational capacities. Although he used various definitions, all centered on the characteristics of the individuals or organizations that committed the crime rather than on the nature of the crime itself. All fit easily with Sutherland's desire to identify criminality in settings where it had previously been ignored. Thus, in his most frequently cited definition he argued: "White collar crime may be defined approximately as a crime committed by a person of respectability and high social status in the course of his occupation."[12]

Sutherland's definition established status, occupation, and organization as the distinguishing qualities of white-collar crime. In the two decades that followed his work, few scholars sought to expand knowledge of white-collar offending. When they did, they focused less on the moral concerns he raised than on the empirical issues he addressed. In particular, interest in crimes made possible because of an offender's occupation increased, while interest in social status declined. The major works included studies of retail pharmacists and meat inspectors, so their authors spoke not of white-collar crime but of "occupational" crime.[13] The offenders studied were not exclusively

10. See, for example, Frederic Thrasher, *The Gang* (Chicago: University of Chicago Press, 1927); Clifford R. Shaw, *Delinquency Areas* (Chicago: University of Chicago Press, 1929); and Clifford R. Shaw and Henry D. McKay, *Juvenile Delinquency in Urban Areas* (Chicago: University of Chicago Press, 1942).

11. Edwin Sutherland and Donald Cressey, *Criminology,* 10th ed. (New York: J. B. Lippincott Company, 1978).

12. Sutherland, *White Collar Crime,* 9.

13. See Newman, "White-Collar Crime," *Law & Contemporary Problems.*

of high status, but it was still characteristics of the offenders that defined whether they were seen as white-collar criminals.

Many in the social sciences hailed Sutherland's idea as a landmark, but many in law and business attacked it.[14] The controversy centered on the identification of violations that were not treated in the criminal law as crimes, and the willingness of Sutherland to define as criminals those who never experienced criminal sanctions. The "crimes" examined in his classic book—such as restraint of trade, violations of patents, unfair labor practices, violations of food and drug acts—were rarely prosecuted in criminal courts. Indeed, they were often violations of administrative rules or simply contract cases resolved in civil court. Although Sutherland identified them as serious moral transgressions and others continue to use his broad definition of criminal conduct,[15] many in the legal community argued that offenses not prosecuted through the criminal law cannot be placed in the same category as those that are.

The attention to white-collar crime that Sutherland demanded would not arise until the early 1970s. The disclosures of corruption at the highest levels of government, evidenced in the Watergate scandals, investigations of American corporations for bribery of foreign officials, and prosecutions of major American manufacturers for the

---

For a discussion of the concept of "occupational crime," see Earl R. Quinney, "The Study of White Collar Crime: Toward a Reorientation in Theory and Research," *Journal of Criminal Law, Criminology, and Police Science* 55 (1964):208–14. Examples of research in this area include Earl R. Quinney, "Occupational Structure and Criminal Behavior: Prescription Violation by Retail Pharmacists," *Social Problems* 11 (1963):179–85; and Frank E. Hartung, "White-Collar Offenses in the Wholesale Meat Industry in Detroit," *American Journal of Sociology* 56 (1950):25–34.

14. See, for example, Paul W. Tappan, "Who Is the Criminal?" *American Sociological Review* 12 (1947) 96–102; Leonard Orland, "Reflections on Corporate Crime: Law in Search of Theory and Scholarship," *American Criminal Law Review* 17 (1980):501–20.

15. See, for example, Marshal Clinard and Peter Yeager, "Corporate Crime: Issues in Research," in Edward Sagarin, ed., *Criminology: New Concerns* (Beverly Hills: Sage, 1979). John Hagan and Patricia Parker, "White Collar Crime and Punishment: The Class Structure and Legal Sanctioning of Securities Violations," *American Sociological Review* 50:302–16; Coleman, *The Criminal Elite* (1989); Steve Blum-West and Timothy J. Carter, "Bringing White-Collar Crimes Back In: An Examination of Crimes and Torts," *Social Problems* 30 (June 1983):545–54.

production of unsafe products for consumers shocked the American public. Concern for white-collar crime exploded, enough so that it could fairly be labeled a social movement.[16] Prosecutors began to give white-collar crimes a high priority, and the federal government invested in research for its study.

For scholars, it was again both moral and theoretical concerns that brought them to the problem of white-collar crime. Many questioned, as Sutherland had years earlier, how researchers could virtually ignore the misdeeds of the rich when the damage of their crimes was often much greater than that of common criminals.[17] Others argued that the predominant emphasis on sexual and social deviation of the 1960s had run its course and that it was time for social scientists to shift their concerns to crimes of complexity and organization.[18]

The study of white-collar crime now included a diverse set of criminal activities, among them bank embezzlement, land swindles, price-fixing, fraudulent loan applications, and bribery. It was not the offender's occupational position or social status that linked these crimes but rather how they were committed. In one influential statement of this new focus, Herbert Edelhertz, a federal prosecutor in the Department of Justice who was to play a major role both in prosecution of white-collar crime and in its scholarly definition, argued that a white-collar crime was "an illegal act or series of illegal acts committed by nonphysical means and by concealment or guile, to obtain money or property, or to obtain business or personal advantage."[19] This conception, which shifted the major focus from the status of the

16. Jack Katz, "The Social Movement against White-Collar Crime," 161–84, in Egon Bittner and Sheldon L. Messinger, eds., *Criminology Review Yearbook*, vol. 2 (Beverly Hills: Sage, 1980).

17. See, for example, Alexander Liazos, "The Poverty of the Sociology of Deviance: Nuts, Sluts, and Preverts [sic]," *Social Problems* 20 (Summer 1972):103–20.

18. See, for example, Stanton Wheeler, "Trends and Problems in the Sociological Study of Crime," *Social Problems* 23 (1976):525–34; Albert J. Reiss, "The Study of Deviant Behavior: Where the Action Is," *Ohio Valley Sociologist* 25 (1966):308–23.

19. Herbert Edelhertz, *The Nature, Impact and Prosecution of White Collar Crime* (Washington, D.C.: U.S. Department of Justice, Law Enforcement Assistance Administration, National Institute of Law Enforcement and Criminal Justice, 1970), 3.

offender to a particular kind of offense, dominated the vision of scholars and federal funding agencies during the 1970s.

The 1980s brought two other major approaches to the fore. One is the development of class-based analyses of American society that have led some to revise Sutherland's original conceptualization of status to include questions of class structure and conflict.[20] These scholars argue that concepts of prestige and status that focus on how individuals are perceived in society fail to capture the ingredients of power and position that make white-collar crimes possible. In their view, concern should center upon the structural positions of white-collar offenders, their control over property and people, and the ways in which those positions allow some to carry out white-collar crimes.

A second approach focuses not on behavior or persons but on the harms that organizations can cause to the environment or individuals. Its central concern is actions taken by public officials or other agents of legitimate organizations that have serious negative physical or economic impact on employees, consumers, or the general public.[21] These harms are often defined by administrative regulations. Thus, the early debates over Sutherland's definition of white-collar crime (and the appropriateness of the criminal label as applied to activities pursued in administrative or civil courts) re-emerge, as does Sutherland's moral critique of American business and society.

The evolution of the concept of white-collar crime has thus been marked by changes in meaning that often preserve rather than reduce fundamental ambiguities. To some, the term still denotes crimes

20. For example, see Gilbert Geis, "White Collar and Corporate Crime," 137–66, in Robert F. Meier, ed., *Major Forms of Crime* (Beverly Hills: Sage, 1984); Hagan and Parker, "White Collar Crime and Punishment"; John Hagan and others, *Structural Criminology* (New Brunswick: Rutgers University Press, 1989).

21. See, for example, Laura Shrill Schrager and James F. Short, Jr., "Towards a Sociology of Organizational Crime," *Social Problems* 25 (1978):407–19; and Diane Vaughan, *Controlling Unlawful Organizational Behavior: Social Structure and Corporate Misconduct* (Chicago: University of Chicago Press, 1983). Ralph Nader provided a more popular tone for this argument in his classic book *Unsafe at Any Speed: The Designed-in Dangers of American Automobiles* (New York: Grossman, 1965). Among recent cases, the sale of Ford Pintos, even after serious design defects became known to company executives, is perhaps the most well known (see Mark Dowie, "Pinto Madness," in Jerome H. Skolnick and Elliot Currie, eds., *Crisis in American Institutions* [Boston: Little, Brown, 1979]).

committed by individuals of high social status. To others, it refers to illegalities committed by organizations or by offenders in certain occupations. For others, the moral domain shapes the way in which white-collar crime is studied. We wanted to develop a sample of white-collar offenders that would be broad enough to allow us to critically explore each of these underlying themes in the study of white-collar crime.

Identifying White-Collar Offenders

Our practical problem was to identify offenders who had been prosecuted for crimes that would be identified by most scholars and laypersons as fitting within a broad definition of white-collar crime. Our first choice was to center our research in the federal judicial system, since it is generally recognized that white-collar crimes constitute a much larger proportion of prosecutions in federal courts than is the case in state or local courts. Within the federal system we selected for our study eight specific statutory offenses that we believed would be included in most conceptions of white-collar crime.[22]

The most obvious choices were those that virtually any American would regard as quintessential white-collar crimes. Criminal violations of securities laws and antitrust laws fall within this category.[23]

---

22. We selected these from the hundreds of sections of the United States Code. The vast majority of offenses were eliminated from consideration on inspection. These include various forms of homicide, robbery, assault, burglary, auto theft, and sex offenses. We also ruled out those statutes primarily designed to control organized crime, for example, the Hobbs Act and criminal RICO statutes.

Categories that had a primarily political dimension were also eliminated, although many of these offenses also have an economic dimension. These include violations of nationality laws, immigration statutes, the selective service act and other acts designed to protect national defenses and violations of the civil rights statutes. Finally, we eliminated a number of miscellaneous categories that might conceivably offer crimes with white-collar characteristics, but where the probability of their doing so was mixed at best and the conduct itself was potentially rare or exotic. In this category are included the specific statutes governing the importation of animals and birds, the transportation of strike breakers, and various maritime and shipping offenses.

23. Securities 15 USC 77–78; Antitrust 15 USC 1–3.

These violations more often than others have become the focus of special federal white-collar-crime task forces and are the subjects of much legal and scholarly discussion of white-collar crime. Presentations of white-collar crime in scholarly publications or the press typically refer to these offenses.

The social movement against white-collar crime was largely a response to the misuse of public authority. Influence gained in federal and state government by private persons who traded money or goods for favors of government officials is often the source of public outrage over white-collar crime. Another of our offenses, bribery, thus includes a number of elements associated with the conceptualizations of white-collar crime described above, including the abuse of public trust.[24]

A fourth white-collar crime is bank embezzlement.[25] The federal bank embezzlement statute applies to officers, directors, agents, tellers, or other employees and almost always involves people committing an offense against the banks that employ them. The abuse of financial trust through the use of special occupations places bank embezzlement in the white-collar crime category.

Of all federal white-collar offenses, our fifth offense, mail and wire fraud, covers the widest variety of wrongs. The mail-fraud and wire-fraud statutes[26] may be used to prosecute any crimes in which the postal service or other federally regulated communication systems are used to defraud individuals or organizations. Since many of the most important financial transactions require the use of mail or wire communications, almost any fraudulent transaction can become a case of mail fraud.

In addition to these five statutory categories, we examined three other violations of federal law, all of which involve fraud or misrepresentation: tax fraud, false claims and statements, and credit fraud. The Internal Revenue Code is one of the most broadly applicable criminal statutes since every income-earning person is subject to its provisions, as are organizations that withhold taxes for their employees.[27] Because people in the highest income brackets have the

24. Bribery 18 USC 201.
25. Bank Embezzlement 18 USC 656.
26. 18 USC 1341 and 18 USC 1343.
27. Violations of the Internal Revenue Service Code are most often prosecuted under 26 USC 7201 (for tax evasion), 7203 (for failure to file, maintain

most to gain from tax fraud, such offenses are often thought of as especially prevalent in the white-collar and professional population.

As federal programs have expanded over a wider range of activities, the federal government has become the source of financing for an extraordinary variety of purposes. This has led to the use of government programs as a locus for the commission of financial fraud. As a result, many sections of the federal criminal code, particularly those concerning false claims upon or against the United States, or departments or agencies thereof, and the making of false, fictitious, or fraudulent statements, are employed to address these crimes.[28] These crimes take advantage of new opportunities for criminality. They often entail both use of occupational position and violation of public trust.[29]

Our final category is credit- or lending-institutions fraud: knowingly making a false statement on loan and credit applications to federally insured financial institutions.[30] Like false claims and statements, these crimes involve fraudulent submissions to organizations. In this society, whose economy runs on credit, it seems natural that the submission of fraudulent applications for loans is an important form of nonviolent economic crime.

These eight crime categories—securities fraud, antitrust violations, bribery, bank embezzlement, postal and wire fraud, false claims and statements, credit- and lending-institution fraud, and tax fraud—comprise our selection of white-collar crimes. We make no claim that they are strictly representative of the total body of white-collar offenses. We are convinced, however, within the limits to be discussed that these eight offenses provide a broad and heterogeneous view of the white-collar criminal activity that is prosecuted in the federal courts. They also provide an unusual opportunity to address the major concerns that have been raised concerning the nature of white-collar criminal behavior and the responses it receives in our criminal justice system.

---

required records, or pay taxes), and 7206 (for false or fraudulent statements to the Internal Revenue Service).

28. False Claims or Statements 18 USC 287, 18 USC 1001.

29. See chapter 2, pp. 33–34.

30. 18 USC 1014.

Shaping Our Investigation

Among the variety of concerns that led to this study, the problem of describing and classifying white-collar crimes and criminals was given great emphasis. Earlier research had tended to focus upon a perfect type of offender, usually a white male businessman, often one who sits high in the hierarchy of a major corporation. While we recognize that this has become a powerful image in the public mind and that it applies to a number of the most familiar white-collar crime cases, our decision as to which federal crimes should be included in our study was informed by our desire to tell a much more general story of white-collar offending. We set out to provide an empirical view of the variety of white-collar crimes and criminals prosecuted in the federal court system.

This concern is linked to a more general problem that has been raised by many of those who study white-collar crime. Is it reasonable to speak, as the concept implies, of a unitary phenomenon of white-collar crime, or does the concept itself conceal a variety of different types?[31] Is there a continuum of white-collarness of offenses,[32] or are there discrete boundaries that allow us to classify different types of white-collar crimes? Finally, can we so easily distinguish crimes and criminals prosecuted under white-collar crime statutes from those prosecuted for so-called common crimes?

Given the extraordinary range of definitions of white-collar illegality, there is the additional problem of identifying which are most salient in increasing our understanding of this phenomenon. Is it better, for example, to emphasize the nature of the offenders, such as is implied by their white-collar status and the positions their backgrounds allow them to occupy? Or should we focus on the nature of the crime? Or should we treat the two as inescapably bound, as the dancer to the dance?

Perhaps more than any other question, the public has focused

31. For examples of attempts to create broader categories of white-collar crime, see Mitchell Lewis Rothman, "The Criminaloid Revisited" (Ph.D. diss., Yale University, 1982); Susan P. Shapiro, *Thinking about White-Collar Crime: Matters of Conceptualization and Research* (Washington, D.C.: U.S. Department of Justice, National Institute of Justice, 1980).

32. Jack Katz, "Legality and Equality: Plea Bargaining in the Prosecution of White-Collar and Common Crime," *Law & Society Review* 13, no. 2 (1979):431–59.

upon the treatment of white-collar offenders in the criminal justice system. The view that those who occupy positions of high status are treated less harshly than those of lower status is shared by laymen and scholars. A related assumption is that those who come from privileged backgrounds are more seriously affected by the stigma and stress associated with legal proceedings. Accordingly, we set out to examine two major themes common in discussions about the treatment of white-collar criminals: that the social and class positions of such offenders allow them to avoid the most serious criminal sanctions and that they suffer much greater harm in the legal process than do common-crime offenders.

In examining these issues we follow a middle path between two approaches that have dominated prior empirical studies of white-collar crime. Some scholars examine dramatic cases in great detail.[33] Others draw upon the mass of information routinely collected by criminal-justice agencies.[34] The former studies allow for a detailed, close-up view of white-collar crime that cannot be gained in any other way, but they provide an uncertain and inaccurate basis for making inferences about the mass of white-collar offenses.[35] The latter stud-

33. For example, see the discussions of the General Electric Conspiracy in Gilbert Geis and Robert F. Meier, eds., *White Collar Crime: Offenses in Business, Politics, and the Professions*. Rev. ed. (New York: Free Press, 1977); the Equity Funding case in Stuart Taylor, Jr., "Sentences Getting Stiffer," *New York Times,* May 9, 1985, sec. D, 4; the OPM affair discussed by Robert Gandossy, *Bad Business: The OPM Scandal and the Seduction of the Establishment* (New York: Basic Books, 1985); and a case of malfeasance in the movie industry provided by David McClintock, *Indecent Exposure: A True Story of Hollywood and Wall Street* (New York: William Morrow, 1982).

34. See, for example, John Hagan, Ilene Nagel-Bernstein, and Celeste Albonetti, "The Differential Sentencing of White-Collar Offenders in Ten Federal District Courts," *American Sociological Review* 45 (1980):802–20.

35. The cases of a Fortune 500 company caught in a criminal conspiracy, a highly placed movie executive whose illegalities open a window into the inner workings of the corporate world, or one or two men who carry out a systematic pattern of deceit that swindles others out of hundreds of millions of dollars are of interest and warrant book-length treatments precisely because they are statistical oddities. These cases are fascinating in part because they are extreme. Sometimes they shed light on the processes of commission, detection, and prosecution of crimes that are hidden from view. They are only available in those rare instances when the human interest in a case runs high enough to justify a journalist or other investigator spending years of research on a single case.

ies provide representative samples of white-collar criminal behavior, but they often report few details of criminal conduct and only surface features of offender background.[36]

We sought to develop an investigation that would provide something closer to the detail of case studies without losing the empirical generalizability of large quantitative investigations. That our study was initiated by a congressional request facilitated our task by providing access to by far the fullest and best documented body of data on convicted federal offenders, the presentence investigation report (PSI).[37]

PSIS are routinely prepared by probation officers to assist judges in making sentencing decisions. Varying in length from as few as three to as many as twenty pages, the PSI describes the offense of conviction, usually in the words of both the defendant and the prosecutor.[38] Essential material on the background of the case, a detailed description of the defendant's educational, medical, employment, family, and criminal histories, and an overall evaluative summary by the probation officer are usually included. The availability of these presentence

36. A vast amount of information about individuals and crimes exists in the records of police and court activities. These records often serve as the basis for the development of generalizations about crime and its control. In contrast to the case studies, these works usually contain data on all offenders who have reached the same point in the operation of the criminal justice system. In general, each group of offenders studied within this approach may best be understood as having crossed some threshold within this system; some examples of such thresholds are indictment, arrest, and conviction.

Even the most complete of such studies are restricted to "face sheet" information listing the statutory category of the offense charged, the plea of the defendant, rudimentary information about bail and lawyers, and such basic background information as the defendant's age, race, and sex. Such data can be cleaned, refined, and items combined in various ways to provide the beginnings of serious analyses of criminal conduct, but facts unrecorded cannot be examined, and these records are woefully short on the details about offense and offender necessary to understand fully the nature of criminal acts and actors.

37. Rule 32(c)(1) of the Federal Rules of Criminal Procedure requires a PSI to be made out on all convicted offenders prior to sentence unless, with the court's permission, the defendant waives the report or the court finds sufficient information in the record to sentence the offender. Approximately 6 percent of our potential sample cases had no PSI, according to Administrative Office data we received.

38. The mean length of the PSIS was 11.1 pages.

investigation reports, not normally accessible to researchers, shaped our exploration of the phenomenon of white-collar crime.

Like other matters of systematic criminal record keeping, PSIS are routinely made out for those who pass a certain threshold in the criminal justice system—namely, conviction in a federal court. Unlike the "face-sheet" reports that dominate most empirical studies, the PSIS are based on hours of detailed collection of information from the prosecution, the defendant, and often from other federal agencies. The narrative accounts of offenses are sometimes as brief as a sentence or two, but they frequently run to two or three pages that provide rich detail on the nature of the underlying conduct and how the misdeed was carried out. Even the routine material on the defendant goes far beyond surface accounts in its description of employment history, family background, and prior record. PSIS may also allow a unique glimpse into an offender's view of the offense and the effects of being processed as a defendant.

Of course, this information is filtered through the eyes of probation officers and may be subject to whatever biases they bring to their work.[39] Nonetheless, the PSIS provide the potential for an analysis of offenses and offenders that begins to approximate the richness of some case studies, but that can be carried out for the vast majority of convicted defendants.

The data that are analyzed in the chapters that follow are based on close readings of presentence investigations for a sample of offenders convicted by either plea or trial of one of our eight white-collar crimes in seven federal districts during fiscal years 1976, 1977, and 1978.[40] The districts were chosen in part to provide geographic diver-

39. Because of the important role the PSIS play in sentencing and the fact that they can be challenged either by defense or prosecution we suspect that they provide fairly reliable information. At the same time we recognize that in going beyond reporting of "facts" about the offense or the offender's background we can be much less sure of the PSIS' accuracy. In subsequent chapters we draw attention to these difficulties and illustrate some inconsistencies we found in the information provided.

40. The sample was selected from data maintained by the Administrative Office of the United States Courts. Of all PSIS we requested, we received 86 percent. Our largest underrepresentation by district was in Northern Illinois, where files were often kept in local offices.

Check coding was completed for 119 cases. This represents 10 percent of the first 100 cases completed by each coder, and 5 percent thereafter. All the

sity, in part because they were being examined in other studies, and in part because some of them were known to have a significant amount of white-collar prosecution.[41] The districts (and their central cities) are Central California (Los Angeles), Northern Georgia (Atlanta), Northern Illinois (Chicago), Maryland (Baltimore), Southern New York (Manhattan and The Bronx), Northern Texas (Dallas), and Western Washington (Seattle).

We chose not to include all the offenders convicted of our eight statutory categories within these districts. Our desire to examine each PSI with an eye to detailing the backgrounds of offenders, as well as the crimes they had committed, was the major reason for this decision. Only a sample of criminals in each district would allow such a detailed review. At the same time, we knew at the outset that a simple random sample would likely yield many more tax violations and postal frauds than other crimes, and many fewer bribery, antitrust, and securities cases. This is because the former are more common than the latter in the federal system. For this reason we chose to examine a maximum of thirty offenders per type of crime in each of the seven districts. This stratified sample, which is described in Appendix 1, maximized our ability to provide detailed description of each of the offenses.

While this sample forms the primary focus of our analysis, we also collected data on three other groups of offenders (see Appendix 1). Because securities fraud and antitrust cases have generated so much scholarly interest and public concern (and because they occur so infrequently in even the largest individual districts), we studied all offenders convicted of these two crimes in all federal districts during the three fiscal years we examined. We also identified and examined codefendants involved in the cases that fell in our sample. We sought

---

measures used in this analysis were highly reliable, with error rates generally below 0.10.

41. While we chose our districts precisely because they evidence substantial numbers of white-collar prosecutions, we recognize that experience with white-collar crime itself may have impact upon the ways in which particular districts prosecute and sanction offenders (see Michael L. Benson and Esteban Walker, "Sentencing the White Collar Offender," *American Sociological Review* 53 [1988]:294–302). Nonetheless, given the rarity of many forms of white-collar crime, it was crucial that we examine those districts where white-collar prosecutions were most likely to be found.

to learn more about how different individuals involved in the same case were treated.[42]

We also wanted to compare our sample of white-collar criminals with a comparison group of nonviolent, financially oriented common criminals.[43] Our effort to do this was complicated by the fact that most crimes that would fit our definition—run-of-the-mill burglaries and larcenies, for example—are governed by state rather than federal law. The very traits that make the federal system an ideal hunting ground for white-collar crime make it a difficult place for locating a comparison sample of common criminals. Our solution was to choose two related forms of theft—postal theft and postal forgery—that are fairly common throughout the federal system.[44] Postal-theft cases generally involve theft of government-issued checks for welfare or social-security benefits, often from mailboxes on the day they arrive. The primary distinction between postal theft and postal forgery is simply whether the offender is caught at the time of the theft or when he or she tries to cash the check by forging the endorsement of the recipient.[45] We examined fifteen offenders convicted of each of these crimes in each of the seven districts included in our study.

What We Missed

The following chapters will report in detail on the offenders and offenses in our white-collar-crime sample. We think that the sample was carefully devised to provide an extraordinary amount of

42. One of us, Elin Waring, is in the process of examining the phenomenon of co-offending in much more detail than we are able in this book.

43. While recent perspectives have recognized that white-collar crimes can cause physical harm (see Albert J. Reiss, Jr., and Albert Biderman, *Data Sources on White-Collar Law Breaking* [Washington, D.C.: GPO, 1980]), the vast majority do not.

44. These are prosecuted under 18 USC 1708 and 18 USC 495, respectively.

45. Although the two crime types are similar, there are small but systematic differences between them, in the direction one might expect. The forgery offenders are slightly less likely to be unemployed and to have a prior criminal record and are generally better educated. This is not surprising, since forgery has a rudimentary element of fraud and misrepresentation that is lacking in garden variety thefts.

information about white-collar crime and criminals. But implicit in our description of what kinds of cases we include is a statement of what we are missing. Rather than remind the reader at each point that our sample is necessarily limited in some respects, we present those limitations at the outset and trust that the reader will keep them in mind at each step along the way. What we missed falls roughly into four groups.

First, there are other federal white-collar crimes that arguably might have been included in our study. Perjury, bankruptcy fraud, and conspiracy are examples of these. Each may include components of white-collar crime that we have discussed, such as high status or fraudulent conduct. Though the crimes excluded were seen as deficient for our study in one dimension or another,[46] it is quite possible that they present unique and special attributes that we are unable to study in our sample.

A second group of omissions includes violations of either civil or administrative law. The question of whether these are crimes at all has been a point of debate since Sutherland's day, though they continue to be included by some social scientists in samples of white-collar crime. We do not examine these offenses, and we can say little about similar crimes that have only recently become the subject of felony prosecutions, such as environmental and health-related violations associated with the Environmental Protection Act and the Occupational Safety and Health Act.

The case of civil and administrative penalties applied to categories of crime similar to those we studied raises a more difficult question. How is our portrait of white-collar offending biased by our decision not to include administrative or civil penalties attached to such crimes as antitrust violations and securities and Internal Revenue Service frauds? Most important, given the connection that is often made between white-collar crime and elite social status, how does the status of offenders influence the choice of criminal as opposed to civil or administrative prosecution?

Attention to the processing of white-collar offenders through the criminal-justice system has only recently become an explicit focus of

46. In the case of perjury we suspected that many organized crime figures would be found. Conspiracy is captured as a secondary crime in many of our cases, and criminal prosecution of bankruptcy fraud occurs rarely in most of the districts studied.

research interest.[47] Nonetheless, what is known about this process suggests that the relationship between social position and prosecution is extremely complex. There is evidence that those who are highest up the organizational and status hierarchies are somewhat less likely to be criminally prosecuted than others.[48] But prosecutors target more serious crimes for criminal prosecution, and offenders of higher status are more likely to commit such crimes in the first place.[49] Accordingly, though we have no doubt that offenders of higher status would appear more often in a sample that includes civil and administrative actions, the extent of their underrepresentation in our study is offset somewhat by the positive relationship between social position and the seriousness of criminal conduct.[50]

Third, our entire analysis is based on a population of convicted defendants. What we learn, we learn from the losers: those who not only fell under suspicion and were indicted for federal felony offenses but who were also unsuccessful in beating the charges. The problem is hardly a new one to analysts of crime. Indeed, the difficulty of making any inferences about criminality based on those who are caught has been a central problem in criminological study.[51] This problem might be particularly serious in the case of white-collar offending, since victims are often unaware that a crime has been committed.

While we have nothing fresh to say about the problem of the crime that is never detected, we believe that what is known about white-

47. See, for example, Kenneth Carlson and Jan Chaiken, "White Collar Crime," Bureau of Justice Statistics Special Report, 1987; and Hagan and Parker, "White Collar Crime and Punishment."

48. Susan Shapiro, *Wayward Capitalists: Target of the Securities and Exchange Commission* (New Haven: Yale University Press, 1984); Susan Shapiro, "The Road Not Taken: The Elusive Path to Criminal Prosecution for White Collar Offenders," *Law & Society Review* 19 (1985):179–217; Susan Shapiro, "Collaring the Crime, Not the Criminal: 'Liberating' the Concept of White-Collar Crime," *American Sociological Review* 93 (1990):623–58.

49. See Shapiro, "The Road Not Taken"; Hagan and Parker, "White Collar Crime and Punishment"; Michael Benson and Gilbert Geis, "District Attorneys and Corporate Crime: Surveying the Prosecutorial Gatekeepers," *Criminology* 26, no. 3 (1988):505–18.

50. We will say more about this problem in chapter 4.

51. See Albert D. Biderman and Albert J. Reiss, Jr., "On Exploring the Dark Figure of Crime," *Annals of the American Academy of Political and Social Science* 374 (1967):1–15.

collar prosecution and defense suggests that what we learn about convicted defendants will apply as well to those for whom prosecutions have begun but who are not convicted. Some who have studied white-collar prosecution have suggested that powerful business defendants are able to intervene and slow enforcement efforts.[52] Others contend that the professional aspirations of prosecutors may lead them to be more aggressive against the more substantial white-collar crime cases.[53]

According to Kenneth Mann, the underlying criminal conduct of defendants in the cases that lead to conviction is similar to the conduct of those who go free.[54] The difference lies mainly in the vagaries of the evidentiary traces that are left behind; these traces enable some cases to be successfully prosecuted and others not. Although these are necessarily speculative matters, we believe one can learn a great deal about the nature of white-collar crime from a close analysis of convicted cases. This, despite our awareness that the vagaries of federal law enforcement strategies, the overlap of federal and state jurisdiction, and the special nature of some federal crimes all place limits on the inferences that may be drawn from our study.

Finally, we did not include corporations in our sample, though we did examine organizational offending indirectly, through those individuals who were convicted along with corporations. Our choice was largely influenced by our concern with the treatment of individuals in the criminal-justice system, though the fact that relatively few organizational offenders are found in any but the antitrust category was also a factor in our decision. As will become apparent later, access to organizational resources is very important to the white-collar crimes we examine. Yet, our focus is upon individual criminals, and we were not able to examine organizational sanctions, or organizational crimes that do not involve individual defendants.[55]

52. See Coleman, *The Criminal Elite;* John E. Conklin, *"Illegal but Not Criminal"* (Englewood Cliffs, N.J.: Prentice Hall, 1970).

53. See Katz, "Social Movement"; Benson and Geis, "District Attorneys and Corporate Crime."

54. The details of these processes are documented in Kenneth Mann's book in our series, *Defending White-Collar Crime* (New Haven: Yale University Press, 1985).

55. We address these matters in more detail in the concluding chapter.

We have dwelt at length on the varying conceptions of white-collar crime and how these influenced the choices we made as we sought to exploit to the fullest our access to an unusually detailed body of data on white-collar offenders and their crimes. We have done so because our portrait of white-collar crime necessarily develops from these choices. John Braithwaite noted in 1985 that more had been learned about white-color crime in the past five or ten years than in the previous thirty.[56] We believe that our investigation plays an important part in extending this new-found knowledge, but we urge the reader to keep in mind how we chose our sample and how these choices shape our understanding of white-collar crime.

56. Braithwaite, "White Collar Crime," 1–2.

2

White-Collar Crimes

Is it reasonable to speak of a unitary phenomenon of white-collar crime, or does the concept conceal a variety of distinct types? How great is the range of offenses that fall within any legal category, and to what extent do those categories hide commonalities among different white-collar crimes?[1] Finally, is it possible to distinguish clearly between white-collar and common crimes?[2] In the following pages we explore these questions—not by theory or conceptualization but through the close examination of cases in our sample. We begin with a detailed review of each of the eight offenses. We then turn to an examination of the similarities and differences between them, and finally to how they are distinguished from common crimes.

1. This issue has been raised by a number of other scholars, though data for such comparisons have often been lacking. See, for example, Gilbert Geis, *On White-Collar Crime* (Lexington, Mass.: Lexington Books, 1982).

2. This question has intrigued white-collar-crime scholars almost from the outset. Gilbert Geis provides a good review of the debate (Geis, *On White-Collar Crime*). See also George B. Vold, *Theoretical Criminology* (New York: Oxford University Press, 1958), 253; Francis Allen, "Criminal Justice, Legal Values, and the Rehabilitative Ideal," *Journal of Criminal Law, Criminology, and Police Science* 50 (September–October 1959):228; Daniel Bell, *The End of Ideology* (Glencoe, Ill.: Free Press, 1960), 382, n. 42; more recently, Travis Hirschi and Michael Gottfredson, "White-Collar Crime," *Criminology* 25 (1987):949–74.

White-Collar Offenses

The labels that statutes give to particular crimes—for example, bank embezzlement—and even the language of the statutes themselves, provide an ambiguous portrait of what these crimes are actually like. This is especially true for crimes prosecuted under such statutes as mail fraud, which are capable of capturing a broad variety of misdeeds.[3] But even where the law is less ambiguous, the nature of the offenses that might be prosecuted is quite varied. For example, the securities-fraud statute declares it unlawful for any person "to use or employ, in connection with the purchase or sale of any security . . . any manipulative or deceptive device or contrivance."[4] A vast array of activities could fit this definition. An understanding of the empirical realities of these offenses, as opposed to their legal definitions, is a necessary first step in our analysis of white-collar crime.

In conducting this analysis we are confronted by a substantial methodological difficulty that derives from our decision to sample individuals rather than crimes. A sample that begins with offenders may overcount crimes that involve many conspirators and undercount those that involve single perpetrators.[5] In fact, the relationship between crimes and criminals in the sample allows us to move from individuals to cases with comparatively little difficulty. For false claims, credit frauds, tax frauds, and bank embezzlements, very few offenders had codefendants that fell in our basic sample (see Appendix 2).[6] In three of the four remaining categories—securities, anti-

3. See Michael R. Dreeben "Insider Trading and Intangible Rights: The Redefinition of the Mail Fraud Statute," *American Criminal Law Review* 26 (1988):181–228. See also Gary Marx, *Undercover: Police Surveillance in America* (Berkeley: University of California Press, 1988).

4. 15 USC 77–78.

5. Moreover, even if each offense is counted only once, it might be expected that the statistical requirements for random sampling used to gather offenders would not hold for crimes. These concerns do not apply to our sample of antitrust violations and securities frauds because we collected data on all offenders who were convicted. But they are relevant to the other offense categories, where the inclusion of coconspirators could have limited the number of new crimes that were sampled. We would like to thank Albert J. Reiss, Jr., for bringing this issue to our attention.

6. Thus, for example, our sample of 210 tax offenders yields 199 tax cases, and the 201 bank embezzlers make up 187 cases.

trust, and bribery—where codefendants are present most frequently, we generally have the total population of all offenders and thus all cases.[7] The only exception is mail fraud, where the reduction in cases is still less than 30 percent. Thus, we believe that our case sample is representative of the convicted offense behavior in the districts we studied. We use that sample to examine in detail the crimes that fell in each of the statutory categories.

Antitrust

The origins of antitrust legislation have led many to view it as the most elite of white-collar crimes. Near the turn of the century, the activities of oil, railroad, and meat monopolies made "trust-busting" an important political issue and inspired the passage in 1890 of the Sherman Antitrust Act.[8] In the 1920s prosecution of the General Electric company further reinforced the image of antitrust as a crime of successful executives in big business, and indeed almost all of our antitrust offenders are indicted along with a corporation.[9] However, despite the image provided by the best-known cases of price-fixing and other anticompetitive activities, few large companies are involved in the crimes in our sample. Most antitrust conspiracies include small-to-medium-sized corporations, many of which are family-owned or owner-managed. Only a handful issue publicly traded stock.

The antitrust statute is two-pronged—prohibiting, on the one hand, all contracts, conspiracies, and combinations in restraint of trade and, on the other, monopolies and attempts to monopolize. Most cases in our sample fall into the former category. In one case that is in many respects typical of our antitrust offenses, a group of linen companies restrained competition by agreeing upon which companies would work with specific customers. Under their agreement, which was in effect for ten years, businesses that sought linen services for the first time were bid on competitively. However, established contracts were protected. The conspirator handling a particular account

7. The only instance where we do not have all of the cases for such crimes is bribery in the Southern District of New York, where the difference between offenders and cases is relatively small.

8. The statutory definitions of the offenses in our sample are cited in chapter 1.

9. It was the only one of the offense categories in which this was true more than 20 percent of the time.

would notify competitors of its intended bid, thus allowing other companies to submit higher bids. Both meetings and telephone conversations were used to keep the conspiracy going. Although the conspirators employed a number of strategies to discourage the dissatisfied customers of one conspirator from switching to another, accounts did occasionally change hands. Sometimes clients were so unhappy that they could not be dissuaded; in other cases, overzealous salespeople would sign up a competitor's client. Records of such events were maintained, and periodic accountings among companies were made. The conspirator who was "owed" might be referred to a displeased customer of the party that was ahead, or it might be agreed that one firm would take a certain amount of business from the other.

Most antitrust cases, like the one just described, last for long periods of time. Several in our study went on for as long as fifteen years, and almost all lasted more than a year. They also tend to be cooperative ventures, as the statute implies, affecting large numbers of victims. More than 80 percent of the crimes in our sample include five or more coconspirators, and 20 percent had at least one hundred victims.[10] In 60 percent of our antitrust cases the total losses to victims are more than $1 million.

Although the antitrust cases in our sample generally involve large sums of money, multiple coconspirators, and many victims, they do not begin to rival the national trust-busting cases that have been so closely associated with antitrust violations.[11] Most of the crimes we examine involve attempts to fix prices or to limit competition within a specific locality or region (as opposed to nationally). In one

10. For both antitrust and securities crimes our statistical analyses are based on the entire national sample, unless otherwise noted. Where significant differences were found between the seven district and national samples, those are described in either the text or notes.

11. For example, the cases against IBM, AT&T, the National Football League, Apple Computers, or the major oil companies. Some examples of this media coverage may be found in: Charles Byron, "Windup for Two Supersuits," *Time,* January 18, 1982, 32; Thomas G. Dolan, "A Day of Decision" *Barrons,* January 11, 1982, 32; "California's Oil Pricing Suit," *New York Times,* April 20, 1989, sec. C, 14; "Apple Faces Antitrust Action," *PC Week,* March 27, 1989, 77; "No Joy as Raiders Settle" *New York Times,* March 6, 1989, sec. B, 12. An earlier example is "Rockefeller's Giant Is Cut down to Size, 1911" *Centennial Journal 100 Years in Business, Wall Street Journal,* March 9, 1989, 81.

such case, for example, employees of three chemical-producing corporations met several times over a two-year period, agreeing to raise and fix the prices of chemicals for customers in surrounding states and to make specific freight allowances. Prices were raised almost 50 percent. In another typical case, a group of companies that controlled 70 percent of the building-maintenance business in a large city conspired over fourteen years to divide up customers, submit complementary bids for contracts, and compensate each other for contracts lost.

Securities Frauds

Securities violations, like antitrust cases, usually involve large sums of money (often millions of dollars) and continue over relatively long periods. Whereas antitrust activity is dominated by collusion between parties that are supposedly adversaries in the marketplace, securities frauds involve misrepresentations intended to trick unsuspecting victims into poor investments. The securities statutes recognize that deception can take many forms; they are broadly worded, prohibiting the use of "any device, scheme or artifice to defraud" in the sale of securities, as well as participation in "any transaction, practice, or course of business which operates or would operate as a fraud or deceit of the purchaser." Securities, as defined by the Securities and Exchange Commission (SEC), include any investment instrument, from shares in railroad tank cars to shares in publicly traded corporations.

The range of illegal behavior prosecuted under securities violations is very broad. Nevertheless, the offenses may be divided into two types. In the first, defendants sell securities to individual investors for considerably more than their actual value. In the second, legitimate securities are used for illegal purposes.

In cases of the first type, the most common approach used involves misrepresentation to investors regarding the value of stock being sold or the financial condition of the issuing corporation. The sales of leases in dry oil wells, shares of near-bankrupt corporations, and unregistered stock are all examples of this form of securities fraud.

In one case, for example, the officers of a company manufacturing modular housing inflated the firm's earnings in SEC registration statements, annual reports, and related documents. Their purpose was to boost the value of their own holdings in the company and to insure the success of two public offerings of the company's stock. The fraud began when a legitimate underwriter told the offenders that he would not take the company public until it could show after-tax earnings of at least $1 million. To inflate reported sales figures, land was transferred to a corporate shell and to friends of one of the conspirators. In each case a minimal down payment was made, but the entire sales price was recorded in the firm's books. Thus prepared for its public debut, the corporation registered more than one million shares with the SEC for sale to the investing public. First offered at $16.50 per share, the price of the company's stock rose to $34 after just one day. Two of the offenders sold some of their shares for $1.6 million and $1.7 million, respectively, during the first twenty-four hours the stock was traded.

Several cases involve pyramid or Ponzi schemes. In one such scheme victims were persuaded to invest in a purportedly legitimate marketing plan for the distribution of cosmetics. Once enticed, the victims were encouraged to recruit other investors. The cost of entry into this scheme varied from $50 to several thousand dollars. Federal officials estimated that the public lost at least $34 million over nine years.

Alternatively, offenders often try to entice investors by engaging in various "stock-swapping" schemes. Stock-swapping creates the appearance of widespread investor interest in a particular stock, thus artificially driving up its price. Unlike the direct action taken by corporate officials in making misrepresentations directly to the investors, the stock-swapping cases involve securities dealers who establish several nominee accounts that pass the securities back and forth. In time, the stock is sold to the unsuspecting public at a cost far exceeding its actual value.

In one stock-swapping case fourteen coconspirators employed a series of complex manipulative techniques to inflate the price of a corporate stock 500 percent in one year. These included the use of secret stock transfers through Swiss bank accounts, the purchase of stock in the names of nominees and entities under their control through multiple domestic brokers, and the illegal use of inside information. Future investors were then misled by a favorable article in a national investment journal written by someone who was paid off by the conspirators.

In the second type of securities fraud, insiders in the securities industry buy, sell, or otherwise use stocks at their true values, but the transactions themselves are illegal. In most of these cases stockbrokers misrepresent their relationship to the securities involved. One broker, for example, tried to conceal the fact that his firm had violated a New York Stock Exchange rule prohibiting a member firm from incurring aggregate debt of more than twenty times its net capital. To accomplish this he used his customers' securities to obtain loans of $7 million. Consequently, false and fraudulent records were maintained in an effort to hide the firm's true financial status.

As these cases illustrate, most convicted securities brokers act in the interests of their firms. Examples of crimes where brokers act against the firms' interest include a case where the president of a stock-transfer company issued and sold through local brokerage firms two hundred thousand unregistered shares of stock, and another where the operations manager of a securities office used his firm's securities to cover his own losses in the market.

Although most securities frauds in our sample are complex and result in losses of large sums of money, a few seem particularly simple by comparison. For example, one broker was convicted for failing to disclose that he was being paid to push a particular stock. Such payments are legal if the customer is informed of the broker's incentive.

Mail and Wire Fraud

Like securities violations, mail and wire frauds[12] generally involve attempts to trick victims into purchasing goods or services that are either overpriced or nonexistent. Any fraud that is conducted with use of the mail, wire, radio, or television—even if such use is not central to the crime—meets the statutory definition of mail fraud. Because use of these media is so common in the course of both legitimate and illegitimate business, the statute serves as something of a catchall for types of fraud not prosecuted under other statutes and often acts as a secondary charge when an individual is prosecuted under another statute. Despite this breadth, there are general patterns of offense behavior among our mail frauds, as for the other offense categories. These may best be understood by dividing the crimes according to their victims.

12. We use the term *mail fraud* to refer to both mail fraud and wire fraud.

Almost one in every eight mail-fraud cases victimizes only individuals. Schemes to sell land, oil wells, and worthless bags of "rare" coins appear again and again among these offenses. These schemes generally go on for long periods and defraud large numbers of people. Often, investors—the victims—are solicited through magazine advertising or direct-mail campaigns; they then send in their money only to discover, sooner or later, that they have been deceived.

The amount of money involved in these cases is usually quite large: 60 percent of the mail-fraud offenses that victimize only individuals have takes of more than $100 thousand, and one in five have illegal gains of more than $1 million. In one of the more consequential cases, four offenders established three separate companies that formed a "front" for bogus land transactions. The land sold was advertised as a sound financial investment that would appreciate quickly and could be resold at substantial profit. Advertisements also claimed that the lots were being improved (that is, that water and utilities were being provided), that there was a master plan of development for the community, and that a nearby city was expanding in the direction of the lots. All of these claims were false. The scheme lasted for fifteen years and involved the sale of seventy-seven thousand lots to forty-five thousand individuals, with total sales of more than $17 million.

In another case, the conspirators placed misleading advertisements in European periodicals seeking investors for oil and gas wells in the United States. More than one thousand individuals bought securities (called "fractional undivided working interests in oil and gas wells") through the mail. They sent funds estimated to be in the millions of dollars. This money was used to pay prior investors the income that they were led to believe their wells were producing. In fact, the wells were producing only a small fraction of the reported income.

While many of the larger mail frauds victimize individuals, most schemes are directed against organizations (including the government) or organizations and individuals. Typically, employees victimize their own companies. In one representative case, a manager of a local sales outlet conspired with several others over a four-year period to defraud the lumber company where he worked. They sent documents to the central offices claiming that one of the conspirators made large purchases from the company and was thus entitled to refunds on the basis of "volume discounts." The "purchaser" was a fictitious company invented to receive the rebates. The home office lost $159,933 during the course of the fraud.

The scenario in which an "outsider" victimizes a private organization occurs rarely in our sample, and these cases generally net the smallest amounts of money. Usually, the victim extends something of value, in the form of cash, credit, or merchandise, on the basis of false information provided by the defendant. For example, several offenders fraudulently obtained credit cards by misrepresenting employment or using false names on applications. Others opened personal checking accounts under false names. In one of these cases, the offender notarized checks with a counterfeit certification stamp and presented them to local merchants, defrauding at least thirteen businessmen of more than $52 thousand. Another offender, whose crime illustrates the range of victimizations prosecuted under mail-fraud statutes, used phones with so-called blue boxes to make $1,382 worth of calls.

In some cases the victims include both organizations and individuals. Such offenses usually occur when the offender represents the organization to outsiders and thus occupies a "gatekeeper" role for the organization. For example, one insurance salesman persuaded his customers to buy policies but failed to pass on the purchase money to company headquarters.

The government is the victim in one in seven of the mail-fraud cases. In most of these cases government employees organize the illegal action. In one such instance a realty specialist for the Federal Housing Administration of the Department of Housing and Urban Development (HUD) failed to obtain the three bids required for contracts. He also made false statements on purchase orders, obtained kickbacks in return for repair contracts, and falsely stated that uncompleted work had been completed. By accepting a fairly low bid on work to be done, he was able to pocket the difference between the bid price and the price the department paid. He also received kickbacks from the contractor in the form of "reimbursements" for supplies purchased with government funds. All together, the realty specialist gained $12 thousand.

The government is occasionally victimized by outsiders. In one such case, an offender entered into an ongoing price-fixing and kickback scheme that involved contracts granted by the government for the demolition of buildings. The public official got a 5 percent kick-back from local demolition firms who agreed on the lowest bid and the lowest bidder.

Lending- and Credit-Institution Fraud

Lending- and credit-institution fraud consists of the making of false statements or misrepresentations to any of a number of groups of credit institutions associated with the federal government.[13] As in some mail frauds, the victim organization extends something of value on the basis of false information provided by the offender. Most of these frauds victimize banks that are members of the Federal Reserve System or insured by the Federal Deposit Insurance Corporation. Usually, fraudulent information regarding the potential debtor's identity, resources, or collateral accompanies a loan application. Unlike the types of frauds previously described, in our sample employees rarely act without the cooperation of outsiders to victimize the organizations for which they work. It does happen, however, as when one disgruntled bookkeeper, knowing that he was about to be fired, used a phony document indicating that he was a corporate officer to open a checking account in his employer's name. He withdrew $20 thousand before the fraud was uncovered.

Perhaps the most useful way to distinguish different forms of credit- and lending-institution fraud is by examining the types of loans involved. Approximately half of the cases in our sample involve applications for personal loans. These are usually relatively small and the offenses are quickly uncovered, either when the bank conducts an investigation before granting the loan or when the loan goes into default. In one case, the offender sought a ninety-day $2,500 loan. He claimed to benefit from a trust that earned $20 thousand per year. He also declared that he owned land worth $71 thousand. Both claims were false. Another person applied for and received a loan of $6,045 for the purchase of a vehicle when, in fact, he had already applied for and received a loan of $5,200 for the same purpose on the same day. He made one payment on the first loan and none on the second.

13. These institutions include Reconstruction Finance Corporation, Farm Credit Administration, Federal Reserve, Federal Deposit Insurance Corporation, and the Federal Savings and Loan Insurance Corporation, among others.

Credit and lending frauds that involve business loans are less numerous in our sample, but they generally net larger amounts of money and take longer to execute than those involving personal loans. Overall, fraudulent business loans also seem to take longer to uncover. These frauds are generally large conspiracies, and bank employees often participate. In one such case, a bank officer advised people who had loans rejected by the Small Business Administration (SBA) to declare falsely that their businesses were owned by people of Hispanic descent. He personally approved these loans and submitted falsified applications to the SBA in his professional capacity. In return, the conspirator requested kickbacks from the loan applicants. The twenty loans were worth $2.3 million, and the kickbacks were worth $209 thousand.

The most frequently cited victim in our sample of credit frauds is HUD. Most often, houses repossessed by HUD, which are supposed to be sold to randomly chosen buyers, are fraudulently purchased. Usually real estate agents, who are not eligible to compete in such auctions, submit bids on behalf of phony buyers. When successful, these bidders do not occupy the houses, as is required by HUD, but rather resell them for handsome profits.

Another type of fraud against HUD involves the submission of inflated bills or bids for work.[14] Gatekeepers are again found among these criminals. In one case the offender was an area broker manager for HUD. His job required him to determine the market value of homes repossessed on defaulted Federal Housing Authority (FHA) loans and to obtain contractors to do repair work. He bypassed the competitive-bid requirement and arranged to have the work done by "friendly" companies, who paid healthy kickbacks. In another case officers and employees of a contractor billed HUD for $90 thousand in kickbacks to architects, subcontractors, and laborers.

False Claims

It is a criminal offense to make a false claim against any federal agency or to make a false statement in any matter involving a federal

---

14. This type of fraud occurs more rarely in our sample than those discussed above.

agency. As was true for credit fraud, many of the false-claims offenders defraud HUD. There are also many offenders prosecuted for false claims to the Veterans Administration (VA), the Internal Revenue Service (IRS), and the Department of Health, Education, and Welfare (HEW).[15] But some targets appear just once or twice in the sample; they range from the Air Force to the U.S. Marshall's office.

False-claims cases generally involve attempts to obtain something of value, usually cash, loans, or services, for nothing. Only occasionally do we find an example of a prosecution of an individual for false claims when he or she did not seek immediate benefit. This usually occurs when the false statement was made to cover up a separate offense. Few cases involve very large victimizations. More than half of our false claims crimes stood to gain $5 thousand or less.

There seem to be two distinct patterns to false-claims cases. In the first, individuals make false claims on behalf of themselves or other individuals; in the second, such claims are made on behalf of an organization. Individuals and groups acting outside of organizations most often victimize HUD, the VA, and the Social Security Administration (SSA). For example, several offenders claimed that they were entitled to veteran's educational benefits when, in fact, they were not enrolled in approved programs. Others manipulated loan applications to HUD or the VA to secure loans or loan guarantees for housing.

As in other types of fraud, a number of crimes involve a third party within the victimized organization. This third party, often a processing clerk, would place the seal of approval on loans or other benefits, allowing the frauds to be concealed for long periods. In one case involving a Medicaid fraud, for example, the defendant and the codefendant, a claims processor at Blue Cross/Blue Shield, were able to defraud the government of more than $126 thousand over a four-year period.

Several false-statements cases involve very bold IRS frauds. Offenders use fictitious names and have companies submit false W–2

15. An agency whose responsibilities are now divided between the Department of Health and Human Services, and the Department of Education.

forms. They are often backed up by fictitious wage and tax statements from the purported employers. In the most striking case, a career IRS swindler submitted tax statements for Michael Rodent (also known as Mickey Mouse) and his seven dependents (the mouseketeers). This offender submitted as many as eighty-five false claims to the IRS for as much as $77 thousand per year.

Often false-claims crimes in our sample are extremely simple. For example, one federal employee was convicted for filing a travel voucher inflated by $204. In another case, the offender indicated on a job application to the U.S. Postal Service that he had no physical problems when, in reality, he had a back ailment. Later, he sought compensation for a back injury that he claimed was incurred while on the job at the post office. The compensation claim was rejected, and he was prosecuted despite the fact that his attempt to defraud the government was unsuccessful. This was one of several cases in our sample for which the prosecution hinged on job applications. In another, a job applicant said that the only crime of which he had ever been convicted involved "tickets," although he had been convicted of a serious crime. In some of these cases the government seems to have prosecuted people over a seemingly trivial matter when the employee had engaged in another illegal activity for which there was insufficient evidence for prosecution.

In the cases in which individuals make false claims on behalf of an organization, the victim is often HUD or the SSA. The extent of liability incurred by the government in such cases is often quite substantial. In one of the few cases of this type involving an insider in the victimized agency, a VA eligibility clerk working with a real-estate broker provided home buyers with "statements of eligibility" for VA mortgages. Many of the buyers were poor credit risks and were not veterans. Over a four-year period, the VA was defrauded of more than $2 million. In other instances, various health professionals billed Medicaid for overvalued work or work not done. In one case, the offender fraudulently obtained a license to operate a medical laboratory by claiming degrees and experience he did not really have. He subsequently billed Medicaid and private insurance companies for work he reported was done at the request of various doctors. In another case a doctor claimed he had performed work on a patient who was, in fact, dead.

Bribery

The bribery statute prohibits offering, soliciting, or accepting anything of value in return for influence over the actions of a public official. The services that bribes can buy, as well as the forms that the bribe can take, vary considerably. Bribery differs in basic ways from other crimes. Like the price-fixing conspiracy, the successful bribe is inherently collusive. But whereas the collusion of antitrust is one of partners carrying out the same actions, the bribe requires that two distinct roles be fulfilled: briber and bribee. A single statute covers both criminal acts.

A majority of the bribery offenders in our sample are prosecuted for offering bribes. Of these, only four of every ten have had their offers accepted. In some cases, a specific victim of the crime is difficult to identify, especially when the bribe is considered "a part of doing business." Indeed, almost all bribes are paid to people actually carrying out their job responsibilities. As was true in many antitrust cases the victim—especially the general public—is almost always unaware that the crime has taken place until the authorities begin prosecutions.

Most of the bribery offenses in our sample represent attempts to have rules bypassed or waived, and are what Michael Reisman calls "variance" bribes.[16] Most often, these crimes involve relatively small amounts offered to IRS auditors. In a typical case the owner of a small yet successful business being audited offered $500 to an IRS agent for favorable tax treatment. A very different example of variance bribes is provided by employees of a corporation hired by a state government to collect on student loans that were in default. One offender accepted money and a trip in exchange for influencing the governor's actions on an individual's loan status. Another bribed officials of the HEW to receive favorable treatment for the company.

While such variance bribes dominate in our sample, other forms of bribery are represented. A few offenders attempted to secure the continuous services of government employees (what Reisman calls "outright purchase bribes"), and these presented some of the most complex crimes in this offense category. In one such case, a VA hous-

16. W. Michael Reisman, *Folded Lies: Bribery, Crusades, and Reforms* (New York: Free Press, 1979).

ing appraiser received bribes from a real-estate broker to approve houses for VA loans. In another, a nursing-home operator received a series of kickbacks from a drug company in return for dispensing the company's drugs to all of his public-aid patients.

Our sample contains relatively few cases of what Reisman calls "transaction" bribes: cases where an official is paid to expedite a transaction that would have eventually been completed anyway. In one typical scenario, the offender offered a bribe of $1,000 to an investigator from the Immigration and Naturalization Service (INS) to expedite the processing of the papers of an immigrating friend and to obtain his Alien Registration Receipt card. The investigator informed the Federal Bureau of Investigation and met with the defendant while wearing a "wire" to gather evidence.

Tax Violations

Like false-claims and -statements cases, violations of the Internal Revenue Code are designed almost exclusively to prosecute those who victimize a government agency. The agency in this case is the IRS. Our sample of tax offenders includes people convicted of one of three specific felony violations of the Internal Revenue Code: willful evasion of taxes owed; failure to file required taxes, returns, or records or to supply information otherwise required; and making or subscribing to a document or return containing information known to be false.[17]

Most of the tax violators in our sample fail to report some or all of their income, usually with the sole purpose of reducing the amount of taxes paid. Generally, their unreported income is legally earned, and rarely do these individual offenders owe very large amounts of money. Although one tax evader failed to file any returns over a period of twenty years, in our sample offenders rarely pursue a career of IRS fraud. Rather, as was the case with one self-employed doctor who failed to report earnings subject to approximately $1,300 in withholding taxes, failures to file are most often short-term offenses. Underreporting of income seems to be most easily carried out by the self-employed.

One-fifth of the tax offenders fail to report illegal income. These

17. We sampled an equal number of each of these types of IRS violations when possible. Within each district there were at least eight and no more than twelve offenders for each of the three tax offenses.

individuals may be assumed to have violated other laws, and it seems likely that they were prosecuted under IRS statutes at least in part because the government was unable to prosecute them for the other offenses they had committed. In many ways these cases expand traditional boundaries in the study of white-collar crime. In one such case a reputed narcotics trafficker with mob connections was convicted of failing to report income from the sale of heroin and cocaine. A tax conviction was sought because the statute of limitations for drug trafficking had expired. Another offender stole $24 thousand from his construction company, but because there was insufficient evidence for an embezzlement conviction, the government sought and obtained a conviction for tax evasion. A third offender grossed some $10 thousand a day in a bookmaking operation and did not report any of that income. The tax violation was worth approximately $500 thousand.

A small group of offenders reduce the taxes they claim to owe by manipulating other components of the tax procedure. One method they use is the inflation of the number of exemptions claimed. A number of these criminals cite political or religious reasons for refusing to pay their taxes in full. One such "conscientious objector" claimed ninety-nine exemptions.

A final subgroup of crimes prosecuted under tax statutes can be committed only by employers. In this category are convictions resulting from a failure to remit taxes lawfully withheld from employee paychecks. As with other tax offenses, carrying out this crime requires only a simple misrepresentation or omission on forms submitted to the IRS.

Bank Embezzlement

Our final statutory offense, bank embezzlement, is of unique concern to the researcher, because although it may be conducted with "concealment and guile,"[18] it may also be committed in a fashion closely resembling simple theft. According to statute, bank embezzlement occurs when a person who is "an officer, director, agent, employee of, or connected in any capacity with any Federal Reserve bank, member bank, national bank or insured bank . . . embezzles,

18. Herbert Edelhertz, *The Nature, Impact and Prosecution of White Collar Crime* (Washington, D.C.: National Institute of Law Enforcement and Criminal Justice, 1970), 70–71.

abstracts, purloins, or willfully misapplies"[19] its funds or funds it holds in accounts.

Victims of bank embezzlements have something taken from them without their knowledge or consent. In one typical case, a customer-service representative pocketed $350 from a teller's drawer. The teller saw him and notified bank authorities. After an audit, the embezzler was confronted and confessed. In another, the embezzler, who had been employed for ten years as a vault guard, started taking money while on duty. At one point he took a package of one thousand $5 bills. At other times, he pocketed cash given to him by customers wishing to pay for safety deposit boxes. Banks appear to provide their low-level employees with many opportunities to steal, although the amounts of money involved are usually relatively small. In more than half of these cases the illegal gain was less than $5,000.

Not all bank embezzlements are this simple. A number involve large sums of money embezzled by high-ranking employees. In one case, for example, the vice president of an important commercial bank made a series of large loans to foreign shipowners. All participants knew that the collateral was overvalued and that the loan would never be repaid. The bank claimed losses of between $30 million and $60 million.

We found that sources of money in bank embezzlement fall into two general categories. In one, there is manipulation of accounts that belong to an individual investor. In the other, there is illegal activity involving money that belongs to the bank itself. The cases described above fall into the latter category. In an example of the former, one teller issued duplicate deposit slips to customers making cash deposits and then destroyed the original slips. She then pocketed the cash.

Often a simple theft of funds leads to a complex cover-up involving manipulation of bank records over long periods of time. In one such case a clerk transferred funds from the accounts of others into her own. She covered up the crime by transferring money from still different accounts into the accounts from which she had already stolen.

19. 18 USC 565,1005.

The Organizational Complexity and the Impact of White-Collar Crimes

Our review of the individual offense categories illustrates the diversity among them and raises the question of whether white-collar offenses may usefully be seen as clustering into different groups of crimes rather than as a single unitary category. In examining this question we concentrate upon two dimensions of offense behavior that are often cited when speaking of white-collar crime. The first is the degree of organizational complexity used in developing and carrying out an offense. By this we mean offenses that have a discernable pattern, that use organizational resources, that are committed by a number of conspirators, and that take place over long periods of time.[20] The second component has to do with the consequences of the crimes for their victims: how many are hurt, how much was taken, and how wide the impact.[21]

Table 2.1 suggests the utility of this approach. The eight offense categories can be divided reasonably well into three types, forming a rough hierarchy of offense complexity. At the top of the hierarchy are antitrust and securities fraud, where the crimes generally are patterned and repetitive, involve organizations, and include several

20. The specific items used here include: (1) Which of the following comes closest to describing the level of organization of the actual offense: conducted by a single individual; conducted by two or more affiliated persons (a group); conducted through an organized association, business organization, partnership, or family business; (2) Which of the following comes closest to describing the actual nature of the offense: illegal activity happens only once (may include cover-up); illegal activity happens on a number of separate occasions, but not patterned, regular, or related; illegal activity happens on a number of separate occasions but does not seem to be part of an overarching plan; illegal activity involves a number of activities (discrete or continuous) that have one cumulative effect; (3) Duration of actual offense: ordinal, from one day to seven or more years; and (4) Number of additional persons involved in the actual offense: give the actual number.

21. The coders were asked to record the following: (1) Geographic spread of illegality: individual/business (affects only the immediate participants); local (spread over the local community); state or regional; national; international; (2) Number of actual victims: code the number whenever possible, otherwise class as a large or small group; (3) Magnitude of illegality in dollars: an ordinal scale from none to $2.5 million or more.

Table 2.1. Comparisons among White-Collar Crimes (for the Case Sample): Organizational Complexity

Offense Categories	Percent with a Pattern to the Crime $(N)^2$	Percent with Organization Used $(N)^2$	Percent with 6 or More Persons Involved $(N)^2$	Percent with Duration of a Year or More $(N)^2$
High				
Antitrust[1]	97.3%	100.0%	79.4%	75.8%
	(37)	(36)	(34)	(33)
Securities Fraud[1]	94.7%	79.8%	52.4%	67.9%
	(113)	(114)	(105)	(109)
Moderate				
Mail Fraud	78.2%	25.8%	16.7%	48.4%
	(133)	(132)	(132)	(128)
False Claims	58.4%	25.6%	17.0%	52.0%
	(137)	(137)	(135)	(127)
Bribery	50.8%	36.7%	35.0%	38.9%
	(59)	(60)	(60)	(54)
Low				
Tax Fraud	44.7%	14.6%	3.0%	84.3%
	(197)	(199)	(199)	(191)
Credit Fraud	43.9%	21.0%	7.4%	27.0%
	(139)	(138)	(136)	(126)
Bank Embezzlement	37.3%	7.5%	3.2%	24.3%
	(185)	(187)	(186)	(173)

[1] Includes all cases nationwide. See Appendix 2.

[2] The figures in parentheses represent the number of cases with nonmissing information for that variable. For sample size information, see Appendix 2.

people in a conspiracy. Though the two offenses differ in their basic modes of commission, with antitrust depending upon collusion and securities fraud upon systematic deception, they are similar in that both require a high level of planning and organization.

At the other end of the hierarchy are the bank embezzlements, credit frauds, and tax offenses found in our sample. Few of these offenses are committed through organizations. Seldom do these crimes involve large conspiracies. They are also less likely to be patterned

Table 2.2. Comparisons among White-Collar Crimes (for the Case Sample): Victimization

Offense Categories	Percent with 100 or More Victims $(N)^2$	Percent with $100,000 or More Taken $(N)^2$	Percent with Statewide or Wider Spread $(N)^2$
High			
Antitrust[1]	85.7%	100.0%	68.6%
	(7)	(10)	(35)
Securities Fraud[1]	62.9%	85.9%	73.3%
	(35)	(78)	(86)
Moderate			
Mail Fraud	11.9%	25.0%	28.0%
	(134)	(100)	(132)
Low			
False Claims	1.5%	10.3%	7.4%
	(137)	(87)	(135)
Credit Fraud	0.7%	20.2%	5.1%
	(139)	(109)	(136)
Bribery	1.6%	7.3%	8.6%
	(61)	(41)	(58)
Tax Fraud	1.5%	10.4%	1.0%
	(199)	(125)	(197)
Bank Embezzlement	0.0%	7.6%	2.7%
	(187)	(171)	(187)

[1] Includes the nationwide sample. See Appendix 2.

[2] The figures in parentheses represent the number of cases with nonmissing information for that variable. See Appendix 2 for details on sample sizes.

than are our other white-collar offenses. Tax offenses are likely to involve crimes of long duration not because of their sophistication but because most tax reporting is done annually. Despite these inconsistencies, the differences between the offense categories with the highest and lowest levels of organizational complexity are enormous. The other three offense categories—mail fraud, false claims, and bribery—fall between these two extremes.

Examining the nature and extent of victimization presents a somewhat different set of distinctions among the statutory offenses (table 2.2). Once again, securities and antitrust offenses fall at the highest end of the range. They are more likely than other types of cases to affect very large numbers of victims and are the most likely of any of our offense categories to include victimization that spreads across county, state, and national boundaries. In almost all of these crimes more than $100 thousand is stolen.

At the other end of the hierarchy are not just bank embezzlements, credit fraud, and tax violations, but also false claims and bribery. Although there is considerable variation within these categories, particularly in the magnitude of the offense, they share a pattern of harming only one victim (typically a large public or private organization) and yielding a relatively small profit, and they are largely local in their commission and impact. Mail and wire fraud fall at an intermediate level, with more victims, more money taken, and a greater geographic scope.

Combined, the dimensions of victimization and organizational complexity produce a four-level hierarchy of white-collar offenses. Securities and antitrust define one end of the scale. At the other end are tax fraud, credit fraud, and bank embezzlement cases. These crimes are not highly organized and cause comparatively little harm. The three other offenses provide a mid-range of white-collar offending. Bribery and false claims offenses involve moderate social organization and minor victimization and thus fall into a lower middle category. Mail fraud forms an upper middle category of its own, because it involves medium levels of both victimization and organization.

This hierarchy based on organizational complexity and victimization highlights the diversity that characterizes white-collar crime. It suggests as well that we may usefully distinguish between the quintessential white-collar crimes (securities frauds and antitrust violations), those that are generally at the fringes of white-collar criminal behavior (tax offenses, credit frauds, and bank embezzlements), and those that represent an intermediate position (mail frauds, briberies, and false claims). This analysis also raises the question of whether this fairly clear hierarchy of white-collar offenses obliterates the distinction between white-collar and common crime.

Comparing White-Collar and Common Crimes

Our white-collar crimes evidence patterns of victimization that differ markedly from our comparison common crimes of postal theft

Table 2.3. White-Collar and Common Crimes: A Comparison of
Victimization (for the Case Sample)

Victimization	Common Crimes (N)[1]	White-Collar Crimes (N)[2]
Percent with National or International Spread of Illegality	1.0% (193)	7.4% (868)
Percent with 100 or More Victims	0.0% (147)	5.7% (899)
Percent Taking More than $100,000	2.8% (143)	16.0% (657)
Percent Victimizing Organizations[3]	27.9% (190)	94.8% (841)

[1]The numbers given in each cell represent the cases with nonmissing information for each variable. The sample includes 204 cases.

[2]The white-collar-crime sample includes only those cases represented in the basic sample (see Appendix 2). The numbers given in each cell represent the cases with nonmissing values for the variable. The sample includes 899 cases.

[3]Includes any case in which an organization is victimized, including those in combination with individuals.

and forgery (see table 2.3).[22] Nearly all of our white-collar crimes involve some form of organizational victimization.[23] A number are spread across county, state, and national boundaries, and 16 percent involve more than $100 thousand stolen. In contrast, few of our common crimes victimize organizations, and they usually have local impact and little potential gain. Whereas very few of our white-collar crime cases in the seven district sample involve one hundred or more victims, none of the common crimes do.

22. We recognize that, in other forms of crime, victimization measures would most probably include attention to the physical or psychological harm the crimes cause. We take it as a given that white-collar crimes generally do not inflict this type of harm on victims. Our selection of a comparison group of nonviolent economic offenses was also influenced by these concerns. Generally, the harms caused by our common-crime offenders may be measured in a similar fashion to those of the white-collar-crime sample. For a description of these crimes, see chapter 1.

23. In this section we examine only offenses found within the seven-district sample.

Table 2.4. White-Collar and Common Crimes: A Comparison of
Organizational Complexity (for the Case Sample)

	Common Crimes (N)[1]	White-Collar Crimes (N)[2]
Percent with a Pattern to the Crime	24.0% (204)	52.9% (892)
Percent with Crimes Lasting More than a Year	6.8% (192)	49.9% (839)
Percent Using an Organization	2.5% (204)	22.1% (895)
Percent with 5 or More Additional Persons Involved	8.0% (200)	13.0% (889)

[1]The numbers given in each cell represent the cases with nonmissing information for each variable. The sample includes 204 cases.

[2]The white-collar-crime sample includes only those cases represented in the basic sample (see Appendix 2). The numbers given in each cell represent the cases with nonmissing values for the variable. The sample includes 899 cases.

Even the offenses lowest in our hierarchy of white-collar crime show important contrasts with the common crimes we examined. Tax and credit frauds, false claims offenses, bank embezzlements, and briberies are all much more likely than postal thefts and forgeries to involve victimizations spread across states or the nation and to result in profits of more than $100 thousand.

We reach similar conclusions when we examine the organizational complexity of the crimes (see table 2.4). Just as white-collar crimes are more likely to victimize organizations, they are also more likely than common crimes to use an organization in their commission. The common crimes are also much less likely to have five or more coconspirators, and unlike white-collar crimes they seldom involve a pattern of offending. The biggest difference in the nature of these types of crime lies in their duration: only 7 percent of the common crimes lasted more than one year, whereas half of the white-collar crimes did so.

Only in the case of the number of conspirators do the common crimes show greater complexity than any of the white-collar crime categories. And even though postal thefts and forgeries involve five or more coconspirators more often than bank embezzlement and tax fraud, these latter offenses are much more likely to last more than a year, to utilize organizational resources, and to show a pattern of offending.

Our white-collar crimes are thus clearly distinguished from our comparison sample of common crimes. At the same time we recognize that our results are due in part to the particular common crimes we examine. For example, had we chosen drug offenses and organized crime cases prosecuted under the Racketeer-Influenced Corrupt Organizations Act (RICO) statutes, we would have found crimes that were more patterned, more likely to involve organizations, and more likely to go on for long periods of time. Nevertheless, as we argued in chapter 1, we think that limiting our comparisons to criminal activities that involve economic transactions and have a heavy presumption of nonviolence provides the clearest and most relevant basis for contrasting white-collar and common crimes.

Scholars and laypeople often possess a romantic view of the kind of problem that white-collar crime represents. A distinction between "crime in the streets" and "crime in the suites" is a typical part of this view, especially given the recent government focus on such securities mega-crimes as those charged against Ivan Boesky and Michael Milken.[24] These cases may be symbolically important for what they convey about the nation's business and financial leadership, and they are surely the stuff of which novels and popular movies are made. But, as important as these cases are individually, and as influential as they may be within the business and financial community, they comprise only a tiny portion of the white-collar cases processed in the federal court system. This is true whether one examines all the types of white-collar crime we reviewed here or restricts oneself to the top of the hierarchy we have identified.

In either case, we are struck by the banal, mundane quality of the

24. See Connie Bruck, *The Predator's Ball* (New York: Penguin Books, 1988).

vast majority of white-collar crimes in our sample. Even the antitrust and securities fraud cases often have an undramatic, local or regional quality. Such offenses are often serious and involve major economic harm, but they have a common, familiar ring. Simply put, they are business frauds, as familiar in their business context as are street crimes in poor communities.

3

White-Collar Criminals

When Sutherland coined the term *white-collar crime* his focus was upon "persons of the upper socioeconomic class."[1] His concern was to illustrate to criminologists and others that crime was as much a part of the world of successful executives as it was endemic to poor urban neighborhoods. And indeed, both in rhetoric and research, the white-collar offender has been pictured as the polar opposite of the common criminal. As much as we have come to see street crime primarily as the work of disadvantaged young men from broken families and decaying neighborhoods, white-collar crime has been linked to advantaged older men from stable homes living in well-kept communities.

Of course, this is an oversimplification of many of the portraits of white-collar crime that have been drawn by other scholars.[2] Nonetheless, white-collar criminals remain in the eyes of most scholars and laypersons "upper class" or "elite" criminals. In this chapter we examine this image of white-collar offenders in the context of the

1. Edwin H. Sutherland, *White Collar Crime: The Uncut Version* (New Haven: Yale University Press, 1983), 7.
2. See, for example, Hazel Croall, "Who Is the White Collar Criminal?" *British Journal of Criminology* 29, no. 2 (1989):157–73.

offenses we have just described. We begin by examining the types of people who are convicted of various types of white-collar crime. We then turn to the ways in which white-collar criminals are similar or different from both common criminals and ordinary Americans.

Relating Offense and Offender

Our examination of white-collar offenses revealed a hierarchy in which antitrust and securities crimes occupied the upper range and tax evasions and bank embezzlements the lower. When we turn from the nature of the crimes to the nature of the offenders, we find some interesting similarities and differences. In table 3.1, we present background characteristics of the people who commit each type of white-collar crime.

The eight legal categories can be meaningfully reduced to four groups. At the top again are antitrust and securities fraud offenders: middle-aged white males with stable employment in white-collar jobs, more often than not owners or officers in their companies, who are well above average in socioeconomic status compared to other offenders.[3] Of the two categories, the antitrust offenders tend to be richer and are less likely to have had prior convictions, though they are slightly less well educated and rank slightly lower on measures of social standing.

The perpetrators in the tax and bribery offenses are also predominantly white males, although a little more often unemployed, and less well educated than their antitrust and securities fraud counterparts. At the same time, they are generally steadily employed in white-collar jobs, and at least a third are owners or officers in their businesses.

At the lower end of the spectrum are the credit fraud, false claim, and mail fraud offenders. Fewer than half are steadily employed, and a quarter of each are unemployed at the time of their offenses. On average they are less likely to have substantial financial assets, to hold college degrees, or to own their own homes than those in the middle category, and more than two-fifths have prior criminal convictions. These offenders are younger on the average than the others, and they are more likely to be female or "nonwhite,"[4] although white males continue to make up the modal category.

3. These measures are explained in detail later in this chapter.
4. Nonwhites include those identified as "Negro," "American Indian,"

Finally, we have the bank embezzlers, who cannot be easily subsumed under one of these other three groups (though they are much closer to the bottom of the hierarchy than the top). They are far younger on average than the others and are nearly as likely to be female as male. They are similar to the lowest of our three groups in financial assets held, but they are far less likely than those offenders to be unemployed or to have a prior criminal record.

If we compare the rankings of offense and offender we find considerable agreement (table 3.2). But what is most surprising in our view is the extent to which the hierarchy of persons departs from that of the offenses. Mail fraud offenders, for example, tend to lie higher up in the hierarchy of organizational complexity and victimization than might be predicted from their social backgrounds alone. By contrast, those convicted of tax fraud tend to have higher social and professional standing than might be presumed from the usually low level of complexity and victimization of their crimes. We will be in a better position to explore these seeming contradictions when we examine in more detail the offenders that fall within each of these groups.

Antitrust and Securities Offenders

Those convicted of antitrust or securities crimes more closely approximate the traditional image of white-collar criminals than offenders in any of the other crime categories. Overall, SEC violators have a less reputable, more marginal appearance than do antitrust offenders. For example, a typical securities violator, who was convicted of (among other things) selling unregistered stock for the company of which he was chairman of the board, was on his second marriage and rented his home. In contrast, the four company presidents convicted in one antitrust conspiracy all had at least some college education (one had a law degree), were married (to their original spouses) with children, and owned their homes. None of these men had a criminal record.

Antitrust offenders often present a public face of stability and uprightness based on characteristics that can take a lifetime to build, and they do this more consistently than do securities violators. For example, they are the best off financially, with median assets of $613

"Asian," and "Hispanic" on the PSI cover sheet. Nonwhites in our sample were predominantly African Americans.

Table 3.1. A Statistical Portrait of the Hierarchy of White-Collar Criminals

	High		Middle		Credit Fraud	Low		Outside Hierarchy Bank Embezzlement
	Antitrust[6]	SEC[6]	Tax	Bribery	Credit Fraud	False Claims	Mail Fraud	Embezzlement
Demographic Characteristics								
Race (Percent White)[1]	99.1%	99.6%	87.1%	83.3%	71.5%	61.8%	76.8%	74.1%
Sex (Percent Male)[1]	99.1%	97.8%	94.3%	95.2%	84.8%	84.7%	82.1%	55.2%
Age (Mean Age)[1]	53	44	47	45	38	39	38	31
Employment								
Percent Steadily Employed[3]	96.6%	59.4%	80.6%	68.4%	42.2%	46.7%	48.0%	36.8%
Percent of Employed in White-Collar Occupations[1]	95.5%	99.0%	75.4%	81.8%	86.2%	74.4%	77.5%	96.9%
Mean Duncan SEI[1]*	61.1	67.4	56.2	59.9	57.3	52.6	55.7	57.3
Percent Unemployed[2]	0.0%	2.8%	11.5%	17.8%	24.2%	24.8%	25.4%	3.0%
Social Class Owners or Officers[2]	71.3%	68.4%	33.3%	36.8%	31.8%	16.4%	28.0%	15.9%
Industry[2]								
Government	0.0%	0.0%	6.9%	20.3%	1.7%	5.3%	12.5%	0.0%
Professional Services	0.0%	9.7%	16.0%	23.0%	5.0%	31.9%	11.0%	0.5%

Banking	0.0%	4.8%	1.1%	2.7%	18.5%	3.5%	2.9%	91.3%
Finance	11.1%	59.7%	5.3%	5.4%	19.3%	15.9%	16.2%	2.6%
Production or Other Services	88.9%	25.8%	70.7%	48.6%	55.5%	43.4%	57.4%	5.6%
Percent Using Their Occupation in Crime[1]	100.0%	97.0%	15.0%	17.8%	48.0%	54.0%	50.0%	95.0%

Personal History

Financial Standing

Median Assets[4]	$200,000	$57,500	$49,500	$45,000	$7,000	$4,000	$2,000	$2,000
Median Liabilities[5]	$40,000	$54,000	$23,500	$19,000	$7,000	$5,000	$3,500	$3,000
Percent with College Degree[1]	40.9%	40.9%	27.4%	28.9%	17.8%	29.2%	21.7%	12.9%
Percent Home Owners[1]	73.5%	58.2%	57.7%	57.0%	44.8%	42.1%	33.5%	28.4%
Percent Married[1]	95.7%	80.7%	52.2%	67.9%	51.0%	52.2%	51.9%	52.2%
Percent with Prior Convictions[1]	7.7%	25.3%	37.1%	17.6%	45.6%	45.2%	40.5%	22.4%

[1] 98% or more of the individuals in each offense category were used as the base for these figures.

[2] At least 90% of the individuals in each offense category were used in calculating these figures.

[3] At least 85% of the individuals in each offense category were used in calculating these figures.

[4] At least 80% of the individuals in each offense category were used in calculating these figures.

[5] At least 75% of the individuals in each offense category were used in calculating these figures.

[6] Based on the nationwide samples of securities and antitrust offenders.

* For employed individuals only

Table 3.2. Comparisons of Offense and Offender Hierarchies

Offense Categories	Rank for Offense Hierarchy	Rank for Offender Hierarchy
Antitrust	High	High
Securities	High	High
Bribery	Middle	Middle
False Claims	Middle	Low
Mail Fraud	Middle	Low
Tax Fraud	Low	Middle
Credit Fraud	Low	Low
Bank Embezzlement	Low	—

thousand and liabilities of only $7 thousand within the seven districts.[5] Securities offenders are the second wealthiest group, as measured by assets alone. Because of their substantial liabilities, however, these offenders seem less financially secure.

Education is one measure on which securities violators outscore antitrust violators. This reversal is largely a result of the type of occupations that the offenders in each group hold. The small number of professionals among antitrust offenders, and the presence of a number of businessmen who started with nothing and worked their way up, lowers the educational level of this category.

There are many other ways in which an individual can achieve an image of respectability. For example, ownership of a home is a symbol of social standing in American culture, sending out, as Constance Perin notes, a message of stability and commitment to the community.[6] Three-quarters of our antitrust offenders own their own homes. Furthering this image, some 40 percent are described by the probation officer as having good general reputations in the community, 98

5. Assets here include equity in homes and property, the value of all major durable consumer goods, and financial holdings. This is one case where the national and seven district samples differ markedly. We believe that the differences in financial status between the national population and the seven-district sample of antitrust offenders is in part a result of the relatively high cost of living in these districts.

6. Constance Perin, *Everything in Its Place: Social Order and Land Use in America* (Princeton: Princeton University Press, 1977). See especially chap. 2, 32–80.

percent are described as being in "good" mental health, and none have drug or alcohol problems reported. Members of both groups are usually married, but the antitrust offenders are overwhelmingly so and seldom have histories of divorce or separation. In contrast, one in six securities violators have been separated or divorced.

While almost all of the antitrust offenders have been steadily employed in the five years preceding their conviction, this is true of just six in every ten of the SEC violators. Almost all of the offenders in both categories are employed in white-collar occupations, and almost universally they use these occupations to commit their crimes. However, the distribution of jobs differs widely between the offenses. The antitrust offenders work in the manufacturing or in the nonprofessional service sectors (for example, the building maintenance or restaurant industries). While a number of antitrust offenders hold law or other advanced degrees, few are practicing professionals. Virtually all of these criminals are managers of some type, most often at high levels. The SEC violators, in contrast, include many practicing professionals.

Fourteen of the fifty practicing lawyers in the sample were convicted of SEC violations. These offenses all involved the artificial inflation of stock prices, and the attorneys played important roles in the crimes. They served as general counsels and corporate officers or were retained to provide specific legal services, such as preparation of offering statements, registration materials, or SEC reports for the corporations or their underwriters. These lawyers—like most of the lawyers in our sample—tended to be on the margins of their profession, practicing on their own or in small firms or partnerships and having attended less prestigious law schools.

Among other SEC offenders in our sample are six accountants who, like the lawyers just described, monitored the finances of the companies involved and added an aura of legitimacy to the accounting process. As a rule, however, they were only marginally involved in the frauds, often having been brought in after the crime had begun. There are also eight real-estate agents in this group. Only one in five securities offenders are stock or bond agents, jobs directly related to securities trading.

The conceptual connection between white-collar crime and white-collar work is obvious. When Sutherland was writing, white-collar work was uniformly high-status work. Today, because of the explosive growth of low-status clerical and technical jobs in American society,[7] white-collar work is no longer synonymous with high social standing and financial success. Indeed, many white-collar jobs are associated with low pay and little opportunity for advancement. Therefore, to develop an accurate understanding of the social status of our offenders we need to make finer distinctions among their occupations. We can do this by examining both the relative social status and class position associated with occupations.

The Duncan Socioeconomic Index (SEI) is a widely used tool for measuring the social standing of individuals. The index assigns a specific numeric status score to each occupation based on the salary, education, and prestige associated with it. For example, bank tellers are assigned a score of 52.0 and managers a score of 62.0. Doctors, who fall at the top of the index, are assigned a score of 96.0, and truck drivers, who fall near the bottom, receive a score of 15.1. Despite the differences in specific occupations between antitrust and securities violators, the social status associated with the jobs held by these two groups of offenders was, on average, very similar.[8] Although they represent the highest status categories in our study, the average status of both groups is far below that associated with the highest status occupations.

Social class, in contrast to status, is concerned with the actual positions of individuals, rather than their relative social standing. We use social class to divide people into groups based on their authority in the workplace and their relation to the means of production. We identify five class categories: owners (those employing others); petty bourgeoisie (sole proprietors); officers; managers (excluding officers); and workers, including the unemployed.[9]

7. See Daniel Bell, *The Coming of Post-Industrial Society* (New York: Basic Books, 1973).

8. Mean SEI scores are 67.4 for SEC violators and 61.1 for antitrust defendants.

9. This measure was created using three variables in the original data set: the offender's class of worker, position in firm, and occupational title. Class of worker has four categories for those who are employed: government worker, private wage and salary worker, self-employed (in own business) worker, unpaid worker in family business. Government workers were classed as either workers or managers based upon their occupational titles. Those whose class of worker indicated that they worked in their own business were classed as owners unless their positions were sole proprietor, free lance, or

Using this measure, securities and antitrust offenders fall primarily in the upper classes. Almost three-quarters of the antitrust offenders are either owners or officers of the companies for which they work. This is true for 68 percent of securities violators. Very few offenders from either offense category could be placed in any of the lower class groupings.

Tax and Bribery Offenders

The tax and bribery offenders are generally of lower social status than the antitrust and securities violators, but of higher status than the offenders who fall in the remaining categories. For example, a company president—who owned a retail dry goods store with six employees—was convicted of attempting to bribe an IRS agent who was auditing his firm. Although he had only a ninth-grade education, in other ways his profile was similar to that of the antitrust violators described above.

The offenders in these two categories are very similar in demographic makeup. They are mostly white males (though both offenses contain a larger number of females and nonwhites than found in antitrust and securities crimes) in their middle forties. They are also likely to be employed at the time of their offenses and on average have relatively stable employment histories, generally in white-collar occupations. A majority of the tax offenders are either sole proprietors or owners of larger businesses, and few use their occupations to commit their crimes. A relatively large number are professionals. Indeed, about 30 percent of the lawyers and 40 percent of the doctors in our sample commit tax violations. At the same time, lawyers and doctors each made up less than one in twenty of the total tax sample. Two-thirds of the tax offenders work in the manufacturing or nonprofessional service sectors.

---

consultant, in which case they were classed as sole proprietors (petit bourgeoisie). Partners were classed as owners. Private employees were classed as workers unless their occupation title or position indicated that they belonged in a different category. Those with a position of director, president, secretary of the corporation, treasurer, or vice president were classed as officers. Others with occupational titles or positions indicating managerial position were classed as managers. Following Hagan and Parker, "White Collar Crime and Punishment," (*American Sociological Review* 50:302–16) all unemployed individuals were classed as workers. There were no unpaid workers in family businesses in our sample.

Many of the professionals who commit tax violations have troubled pasts. The personal histories of the ten medical doctors in the sample—seven of whom committed tax violations—are telling in this regard. Three had prior criminal records, and their convictions included wife beating, and drunk and disorderly conduct. One had had his surgical privileges revoked, in part because his patients suffered high rates of complications. Another had filed for personal and corporate bankruptcy. One earned part of his unreported income by performing illegal abortions. At the same time many of these doctors lived in homes in exclusive sections of their towns and were considered models of achievement. The bribery category also includes many professionals. Indeed, this category contains a higher proportion of people employed in the delivery of professional services than does tax fraud.[10]

The connection between bribery and tax fraud is often a substantive one, and this is particularly clear when the certified public accountants (CPAs) in the two groups are examined. Fifteen of the twenty-six CPAs in our sample fall into one of these two offender categories, and the ten CPAs involved in bribery were all seeking to influence officials of the IRS. Making up 9 percent of the bribery offenders, most of the accountants are college graduates, though few attended elite schools. Many attended state and city universities part-time, often taking five to ten years to finish. Few were ever employed by the major accounting firms.[11]

As was the case with tax offenders, several of the accountants had drinking problems, and a number had histories of marital instability. It is interesting to note that the briberies we examined did not demand any particular accounting skills, although being an accountant put these individuals into the contact with the IRS, which led to the offering or paying of a bribe. This differs from the activities of accountants convicted of securities fraud.

The accountants convicted of tax violations are typical of the tax

10. By this we mean not only anyone who was a doctor, but also anyone who worked in a doctor's office or hospital. Similar terms apply for lawyers and accountants.

11. For example, Deloitte, Haskins and Sells; Ernst and Whinney; Touche Ross; Price Waterhouse; Arthur Young; Coopers and Lybrand; Arthur Anderson; Peat, Marwick, McLintock-Main. At the time of our study this group of firms was collectively known as "the big eight" accounting firms.

violators as a whole, except that three out of five are former IRS employees, who presumably assumed that their superior knowledge of the tax system would help them to defraud it. It is also possible that the IRS directs increased scrutiny at the activities of its former employees.

In contrast to the accountants in the sample, the six tax preparers who victimized the IRS were all convicted of tax violations. Although not professionals in the same sense as are CPAs, these individuals were certainly white-collar workers and occupied positions of trust and responsibility. All but one operated a small tax-preparation service, usually with poor clients. Most had been in business for only a short time. Several were drug addicts or alcoholics.

A larger diversity of occupations is found in the bribery category than in any other. Among the jobs represented are health administrator, bill collector, hairdresser, police officer, truck driver, and professional athlete. Half of the offenders in the category are described as managers. As we observed in chapter 2, many bribes are viewed by those offering or accepting them as a normal part of doing business.

Tax offenders also include people from working-class backgrounds. "Conscientious objectors," for example, tend to be workers who are not well off financially. They generally reside in rural areas and hold strong, often fundamentalist, religious beliefs. Others who failed to report income that was illegally earned are drug traffickers and organized-crime figures.

Very few tax offenders use their occupations to commit their crimes; as mentioned above, the most notable exceptions to this are the tax preparers. Although tax frauds often involve money earned at jobs, seldom are the jobs themselves used to perpetrate the schemes.

Credit Fraud, Mail Fraud, and False Claims

Credit fraud, mail fraud, and false claims define the next group of offenders. The people who are convicted of these three crimes resemble each other in many ways and are quite different from the offenders described above. In particular, they are less likely to be white or male, are younger, and are less likely to have had steady employment than the offenders previously discussed. They are also less likely to fit an image of the "model citizen" than offenders in the preceding categories. For example, 13 percent of the credit-fraud offenders have histories of barbiturate use, and 5 percent are described in the PSIS as drug addicts. The median net worth of the offenders in each category is zero, and both assets and liabilities are much smaller than the figures for the four offenses already discussed.

The profile of credit-fraud offenders is typical of this group. A quarter of those who had never married are parents; this phenomenon is virtually nonexistent in antitrust, bribery, tax, and SEC categories. Twenty-five percent of the offenders convicted of credit fraud, mail fraud, and false claims were unemployed at the time of the offense; these rates are more than double that for any other of the white-collar crime categories. Many are in difficult financial situations. In sum, these three groups include a significant number of offenders who have some kind of personal or family troubles.

These offenses include people from many walks of life and from a broad range of social classes. Credit frauds include bank officers and financial advisers, as well as insurance agents and real-estate agents. Mail frauds include postal clerks, lawyers, accountants, and doctors, although there is no occupation that dominates. The wide variety of occupations is especially pronounced for false-claim offenders. About one in twelve are doctors or pharmacists, and an equal number are blue-collar workers. The prosecution of the many seemingly trivial false-claims cases described in chapter 2—most notably those involving lying on job applications—may in some part account for this variety.

It is also interesting to note that fifteen practicing attorneys in our sample committed mail fraud. Of these, nine were located in Maryland, and six were involved in a single conspiracy (with a group of medical doctors) to submit fraudulent reports and inflate bills to insurance companies. Four of the lawyers involved in mail fraud had engaged in political corruption or influence peddling. Other attorneys violated the trust given to them by cashing checks written to clients or mixing personal and client funds. Finally, three attorneys were involved in the sale of worthless products through the mail.

Only about half of the offenders in these three offense categories use their occupations to commit their crimes, a much lower rate than that found in SEC and antitrust offenses. For these cases occupation has a less direct relationship to the crimes committed. However, as we noted in chapter 2, gatekeepers play an important role in many of these frauds. Thus, there is a disproportionate share of government employees among the mail-fraud offenders, of banking employees among the credit-fraud offenders, and of professional services and government employees among false-claims offenders.

Almost half of the criminals in each of these categories have prior convictions, and just a third of these are for minor crimes. This rate of prior conviction is by far the highest of all the groups. These offenses also include those with the most serious white-collar-crime records in their past. More than a third of the credit- and mail-fraud offenders with convictions had previously been convicted of a white-collar crime, and some seem to be career flimflam artists.

In one false-claims case, two people who were in the Federal Witness Protection Program as a result of testimony about organized crime figures took up credit fraud under their new identities. Another credit-fraud conviction stemmed from an unrelated major investigation of garment-industry unions. As part of the investigation, this offender was kept under surveillance for several years, and evidence of his involvement in the credit fraud came up as an unexpected dividend for investigators. In yet another false-claims case, a group of offenders made false statements regarding the eventual destination of ten thousand submachine guns manufactured in this country. They claimed the weapons were to be exported, when in fact they were going to be sold to organized crime syndicates. These offenders represent a frequently ignored type of white-collar offender, sometimes but not always connected to organized crime, for whom white-collar crime is just one part of a broader criminal career.

Bank Embezzlers

Persons convicted of bank embezzlement are generally quite different from those in other offense categories. Most are closer in background characteristics to those just discussed than to antitrust or securities criminals. The bank embezzlers are the youngest group of offenders, and most likely to be female. They usually come from stable working families without a great deal of money. Almost all of the bank embezzlers are bank employees, and they use their jobs to commit their crimes.

Among bank embezzlers there is a stark contrast between the positions that men and women occupy. Most men are managers or officers in the banks for which they work, though they often have only local managerial responsibilities. Most female bank embezzlers are bank tellers or hold other clerical positions. Clearly, banks provide clerical workers and low-level managers with many opportunities for white-collar crime. There is a fair amount of trust allotted to them, even though they hold relatively low-level jobs.

Interestingly, on one measure of education—high school graduation—the bank embezzlers are among the highest scoring groups, while on another—college graduation—they are the lowest. Whereas bank embezzlers rank relatively high on the SEI, on average they are least likely to own their own homes. Few bank embezzlers have prior criminal convictions, but this may be in great part due to the special character of employment background checks conducted by banking institutions.[12] Here, as with other demographic characteristics, bank embezzlers hold a mixed position, appearing highly respectable in some ways but often holding positions of low social standing.

The Importance of Organizational Position

Examination of the types of offenders in each of the statutory categories and the crimes they commit leads us to a general conclusion about the relationship between white-collar crimes and criminals. The most consequential white-collar crimes—in terms of their scope, impact, and cost in dollars—appear to require for their commission that their perpetrators operate in an environment that provides access to both money and the organizations through which money moves. The status or prestige of the organization, or of the individual who inhabits it, is only an incidental feature, for the key factor is location in the organization where money is to be found.[13]

Of course, merely working in an organization does not, of itself, provide access to the institution's resources. As is apparent from our

12. We are surprised that such a large number of bank employees with criminal records could be hired. There is not a clear indication in the PSIs as to whether these defendants lied on employment forms or were seen as rehabilitated.
13. There are many such organizations that are otherwise unremarkable: state and federal agencies with multimillion dollar budgets, private companies with huge cash flow businesses, organizations whose clients may not be individually wealthy but who are worth many millions in the aggregate.

examination of antitrust and securities offenders, those who have positions as managers, officers, or owners are better situated (and perhaps more often called upon) to commit serious white-collar offenses than are lower level employees. A crucial way in which offender traits such as high social status and education are linked to the degree of victimization is that such characteristics provide access to positions with greater potential for large-scale offending. Where high echelon positions can be occupied without passing hurdles of education and professional training—through promotions from within the agency or company, for example—we would expect to find individuals of lower social status committing a greater number of financially rewarding crimes.

Status and prestige may also have value beyond their role in obtaining advantageous organizational positions. As we have seen in the descriptions above, they may lend the appearance of legitimacy, and thus make it easier for white-collar offenders to obtain money from unsuspecting victims.[14] Status may also be used to help offenders avoid detection, as in the case of accountants who are brought in long after a crime has begun in order to provide a stamp of legitimacy to certain frauds.

If we are right, this means that high status in society should sometimes aid in the commission of crimes of the largest magnitude, but it will seldom be enough in itself. The position conferred by status, rather than status itself, empowers the offender. Accordingly, persons in key positions (with access to the flow of money) whether or not of high status, should have the greatest potential for committing the most harmful offenses. That potential would be limited, however, for those outside of such positions, even when their status in society and their occupational prestige is high.

While we will explicitly test these hypotheses about the relationship between white-collar crimes and criminals in the context of multivariate statistical models in chapter 4, our descriptive observations here provide an explanation for the differences we found in the hierarchies of offense and offender. Tax evasion sits at the lower end of the offense hierarchy because convicted tax offenders seldom use

14. See Robert Gandossy, *Bad Business: The OPM Scandal and the Seduction of the Establishment* (New York: Basic Books, 1985), describing a case where offenders go to great trouble to create a positive impression by moving offices to a prestigious address.

organizational position or organizational resources to carry out their crimes. At the same time, tax offenders have relatively high social standing. Mail fraud, on the other hand, occupies a relatively high position in the offense hierarchy, even though offenders in this category rank lower on most social background characteristics. In this case, the crimes are generally committed through organizations, though the organizations themselves are often bogus or criminal. Although they may assume the trappings of high prestige as a sales gimmick, such organizations do not demand elements of status or professionalism as entry criteria.

White-Collar Offenders as Average Americans

Given the range and variety of offenders that fall into the statutory categories, it is perhaps inconsistent to argue that they may be grouped together and seen as a population distinct from common-crime offenders. Yet, as the discussion below will illustrate, the differences between common and white-collar criminals are in fact much greater than any distinctions between the white-collar crime categories themselves. At the same time, it would be misleading to think of white-collar offenders as a mirror image of common criminals, occupying social and economic positions as far up the societal ladder as common offenders are down it. Indeed, white-collar criminals are generally much closer in background to average Americans than to those who occupy positions of great power and prestige.

Work and Education

It is probably not surprising to learn that fewer than 8 percent of our white-collar offenders were unemployed when they committed their crimes, since the commission of so many of their offenses depends on the offender's occupational position (table 3.3). The general unemployment rate for Americans in the seven districts during the study period is very similar to that of our white-collar offenders.[15]

15. Data on general population characteristics of the seven districts are taken from the Federal Judicial Center's *Judicial District Data Book*, 1983, unless otherwise noted. Data are available from the Inter-University Consortium for Political and Social Research. Neither the Federal Judicial Center nor the Consortium are responsible for analyses herein.

Table 3.3. Work, Education, and Financial Characteristics of Offenders and the General Population

	White-Collar Criminals (N)[4]	General Public	Common Criminals (N)[5]
Work			
Percent Unemployed	7.2%	5.9%[1]	57.5%
	(1,036)		(179)
Percent Steadily Employed	55.1%	not	10.5%
	(1,029)	available	(166)
Percent in White-Collar	77.8%	51.0%[1]	47.4%
Occupations[3]	(1,036)		(69)
Mean Duncan Score[3]	57.3	38.5[2]	36.5
	(923)		(69)
Social Class			
Percent Owners or Officers	31.6%	not	0.0%
	(1,036)	available	(179)
Education			
Percent High School Grad-	78.0%	69.0%[1]	45.5%
uates or GED	(1,080)		(209)
Percent College Graduates	24.7%	19.0%[1]	2.9%
	(1,080)		(209)
Financial Status			
Median Assets	$11,000	not	$0
	(894)	available	(180)
Median Liabilities	$12,000	not	$0
	(901)	available	(184)
Home Ownership			
Percent Home Owners	45.3%	55.0%	6.6%
	(1,016)		(210)

[1]These figures refer to the 1980 population of the seven districts in the main sample and are weighted to reflect the makeup of the white-collar-crime sample. Obtained from the Federal Judicial Center, *Judicial District Data Book*, 1983, and its companion computer tape (see n. 12 above).

[2]This figure is for adult employed males in the United States in 1972. Obtained from Robert M. Hauser and David L. Featherman, *The Process of Stratification: Trends and Analyses* (New York: Academic Press, 1977) (see n. 14 above).

[3]For employed individuals only.

[4]These figures are calculated using only those members of the basic sample (see Appendix 1) with nonmissing values for these variables. The sample includes 1,094 individuals.

[5]These figures are calculated using only those members of the common-crime sample with nonmissing values for the variable. The sample includes 210 individuals.

This is in sharp contrast to our common-crime defendants (and criminal defendants in general),[16] whose unemployment rate is well over 50 percent. Even if we look at the white-collar crime category with the highest percent of unemployed defendants—mail fraud—only one quarter are unemployed at the time of their crimes.

Almost all white-collar offenders in our sample are employed in technical, clerical, or managerial occupations that the Census Bureau defines as white collar. In this regard we find a substantial difference between our offenders and the general population. As might be expected, given the fact that their crimes often require white-collar occupations, they are much more likely to hold white-collar jobs than are other Americans. The work of the few white-collar offenders who held jobs defined by the Census Bureau as blue collar was often similar to that ordinarily associated with white-collar occupations. Many worked in jobs that allowed a considerable degree of autonomy and responsibility. Most notable here were plumbers or electricians, who in some cases owned their own businesses.

White-collar offenders also hold jobs with higher prestige than that of the general population,[17] though, on average, our defendants do not occupy positions of the highest prestige. The types of people who are often popularly associated with white-collar crime—accountants (SEI = 76.8), bank officers (SEI = 79.5), and lawyers (SEI = 92.3)—all have scores considerably higher than the average white-collar offender in our sample. While such professionals are found in large numbers, managers (SEI = 62.0) and bank tellers (SEI = 52.0) are much more numerous.

As would be expected, the contrast between the class positions of our white-collar and our nonviolent common-crime offenders is sharp. Few common-crime offenders may be classified as any but workers. In contrast, about 30 percent of the white-collar sample may be categorized as owners or officers, and fewer than 40 percent are workers.

16. For example, see Michele Sviridoff with Jerome E. McElroy, "Employment and Crime: A Summary Report" (New York: Vera Institute of Justice, 1985).

17. The comparison here is between the white-collar offenders and employed men generally in the United States. See Robert M. Hauser and David L. Featherman, *The Process of Stratification: Trends and Analyses* (New York: Academic Press, 1977), 128, table 5.1. The figure presented here is for 1972.

The white-collar-crime offenders are better educated than the general public, whereas the common-crime offenders occupy a relatively disadvantaged position. Almost eight in ten of the white-collar offenders are high school graduates, in contrast to 69 percent of the general public. Among the common-crime defendants, fewer than half graduated from high school. Whereas only 3 percent of the common criminals are college graduates, about a quarter of the white-collar criminals (and 19 percent of the general public) obtained college degrees. Even bank embezzlers, who are the least likely of the white-collar offenders to have graduated from college, are more than four times as likely to do so than those in our common-crime sample. Three-quarters of the white-collar defendants, however, do not have college diplomas and thus lack one of those badges of "high social status" that Sutherland and others sometimes identify with white-collar criminals.

The white-collar offenders are also much better off financially than the common-crime defendants, though they appear to have less economic security than Americans generally.[18] Indeed, the most interesting fact about the white-collar offenders' aggregate financial status is not the value of their assets but the extent of their liabilities. Many of our offenders have the material goods associated with successful people but may barely be holding their financial selves together.[19] A somewhat similar relationship is found when we look at home ownership. Though white-collar offenders are much more likely to own homes than common-crime offenders, they are slightly less likely to do so than the general adult population in the seven districts we studied.

18. The Census Bureau has only recently begun to collect financial information on American families. In 1983 their median net worth was reported as $24,574, which is equivalent to $14,490 in 1977 dollars. See the U.S. Bureau of Census, *Statistical Abstract of the United States: 1986,* 106th ed. (Washington, D.C.: GPO, 1985), 465.

19. Cressey, in his important research on embezzlers, found that the majority of men in his sample had lived beyond their means for some time before deciding to embezzle. See Donald R. Cressey, *Other People's Money: A Study in the Social Psychology of Embezzlement* (New York: Free Press, 1953). The high level of debt found in our sample suggests that Cressey's findings may be generalizable to the wider phenomenon of white-collar crime.

Prior Criminal Record

Criminal background provides an important measure of the public appearance of our subjects and reflects strongly on an individual's social standing (see table 3.4). In crime samples generally, most people convicted of felonies have prior arrests and convictions.[20] In line with this, almost 90 percent of our comparison common criminals have prior arrests, and more than 80 percent have prior convictions. In contrast, fewer than half of the white-collar criminals have previously been arrested, and only a third have previously been convicted of a crime.

The incidence of chronic offending also differed greatly between common- and white-collar criminals, as did the seriousness of past criminal conduct. For the most part, white-collar offenders are much less likely to have either long or serious criminal records. But we should stress here that these white-collar criminals evidence prior criminality to a much greater extent than most practitioners and scholars would have expected.[21]

Indeed, as a group they are approximately twice as likely to have an arrest record as is the national population.[22] At the same time, the official criminal histories of our offenders do not indicate specialization in criminal careers. Only one in four white-collar offenders with prior records have previously been convicted of a white-collar crime.[23]

20. For example, in a probability sample of defendants arrested for various felony crimes in New York City in 1971, almost two-thirds had prior arrest records, and one-third had prior criminal convictions. See Vera Institute of Justice, *Felony Arrests: Their Prosecutions and Disposition in New York City Courts* (New York: Vera Institute, 1977), 1–22, especially 21.

21. This finding has led to a federally supported study of our white-collar criminals which will track their criminal careers until the late 1980s (see David Weisburd and Ellen Chayet, "White Collar Criminal Careers," NIJ grant #88–1J–CX–0046). See also, David Weisburd, Ellen Chayet, and Elin Waring, "White Collar Crime and Criminal Careers," *Crime and Delinquency* 36, no. 3 (1990):342–55.

22. United States Bureau of Justice Statistics, *Report to the Nation on Crime and Justice.* 2d ed. (Washington, D.C.: U.S. Department of Justice, 1988), 40.

23. In addition to our offense categories, any prior arrest or conviction for other tax frauds, personal fraud (veterans and allotments fraud, social security fraud, conspiracy to defraud, etc.), business fraud (bankruptcy fraud, etc.), other business violations (fair labor law, food and drug act, airline

Table 3.4. The Reputations and Criminal Histories of Offenders
and the General Population

	White-Collar Criminals (N)[2]	General Public	Common Criminals (N)[3]
Criminal Record			
Percent with Prior Arrest	43.4%	16% to	89.5%
	(1,059)	18%[1]	(210)
Percent with Prior Conviction	35.4%	not	81.4%
	(1,059)	available	(210)
Of Those with Prior Arrests			
Percent with Prior White-Collar Conviction	28.5%	not	22.3%
	(460)	available	(188)
Percent with Only Minor Arrests	30.7%	not	14.2%
	(460)	available	(190)
Community Standing			
Reputation			
Percent with Good Reputation	14.7%	not	2.4%
	(1,090)	available	(210)
Letters			
Percent with Positive Letters	10.4%	not	3.8%
	(1,090)	available	(210)

[1]From United States Bureau of Justice Statistics, *Report to the Nation on Crime and Justice.* 2d ed. (Washington, D.C.: U.S. Department of Justice, 1988), 40.

[2]These figures are calculated using only those members of the basic sample (see Appendix 1) with nonmissing values for these variables. The sample includes 1,094 individuals.

[3]These figures are calculated using only those members of the common-crime sample with nonmissing values for the variable. The sample includes 210 individuals.

Reputation in the Community

Another measure of an offender's position in the community is community reputation. We recognize that this is a somewhat vague concept and is difficult to measure in any objective sense. It is not a routinely recorded part of an offender's record. But good reputation is

---

regulations, etc.), embezzlement, and all forms of bribery were coded as previous prior white-collar crimes. These include some misdemeanors and crimes prosecuted in state courts.

often associated with the advantages that white-collar offenders are thought to have in the criminal justice system.

When a defendant has an unusual degree of influence or stature in the community a probation officer will sometimes mention it in the PSI. For example, in the case of one tax evader the probation officer felt it necessary to inform the judge of the defendant's record of community service and public responsibility: "Persons in sensitive and responsible positions in the [defendant's] community were interviewed after the defendant stated, 'you may talk to anyone who has ever known me.' It was quite impressive. The overall view given of this man was—decent, hardworking, community minded, and a good church worker." Whereas approximately one in seven white-collar offenders had some type of positive reputation noted, this was said for only five of the two-hundred-ten common criminals (table 3.4).

Not all white-collar offenders have good reputations. One probation officer had the following to say about an antitrust offender: "The overall reputation of this defendant, reported by constituents and peers in this area, has been categorized, among other things as being unethical, untrustworthy, manipulative, avaricious, and a pleasure seeker and at a time when [he] was at what the community recognized as the 'pinnacle of success,' he exhibited an arrogant, belligerent, self-centered attitude, and was impervious to the general public."

One in ten of the white-collar offenders presented favorable letters of recommendation to bolster their image of respectability. But only one in every twenty-five of the common-crime offenders received such letters. Of course, these letters do not necessarily accurately reflect a person's reputation. Indeed, the presence of letters of recommendation may indicate efforts to create the appearance of respectability rather than respectability itself. One securities violator, who according to the probation officer was knowingly involved in a crime netting more than $1 million, received three such letters. One read in part:

> In my opinion, [the defendant] has always qualified as an individual with the highest qualities of performance as to his personal characteristics. [He] has honored obligations during trying economic times that many "respectable citizens" have walked away from. I feel very badly that such a person is enduring such a trying

experience. He has always been so receptive to the needs and the difficulties of others that somehow it is quite sad for me to realize that now he himself is experiencing such difficulties. It is my sincere hope that this fine human being will be spared any more trials and tribulations and that this unfortunate experience will not be shared by his family.

Another commented: "Wholesome he is. Ethical he is. A good husband he is. A warm and loving father he is. A good citizen he is. Kind he is. Evil, selfish, devious—he is not. No more is he perfect than any of us. His mistakes and his misfortunes, I believe, did not stem from greed or a lack of integrity, but from his abundance of trust, sprinkled with youth, inexperience and maybe a dash of naivete." Importantly, these letters, as most of those in the PSIS, present offenders with more "middle-class" than upper-class reputations. They were often seen as hard working, decent, and church going. While there were those who were described as pillars of the community, more often than not the reputations imputed to these defendants fit those of average Americans.

Sex, Race, Age, and Religion

It is well known that crime is largely a male phenomenon, and this is surely true of white-collar crime as well (table 3.5). While more than 80 percent of the offenders in our eight white-collar categories are male, the number of women is still higher than that found in most studies examining convicted defendants.[24] Interestingly, women constituted an even larger portion of our common-crime sample, an anomaly that results, we believe, from our choice of a nonviolent economic crime sample for comparison.

While it is clear that women are well represented in our white-collar-crime sample, we find few women who commit crimes that lie at the very top of the white-collar crime hierarchy. Indeed, detailed review of the crimes committed by men and women in our sample reveals a general pattern in which women are much less likely than

24. In 1971, for example, only about 9 percent of all persons convicted of serious crimes were women, yet they make up almost 15 percent of our white-collar crime sample. See Rita J. Simon, *The Contemporary Woman and Crime* (Washington, D.C.: GPO, 1975), 64–68.

Table 3.5. Demographic Characteristics of Offenders and the
General Population

	White-Collar Criminals (N)[5]	General Public	Common Criminals (N)[6]
Male (Percent)	82.5% (1,094)	48.6%[1]	68.6% (210)
White (Percent)	77.9% (1,094)	76.8%[2]	34.3% (210)
Age (Mean)	40 (1,093)	30[1]	30 (210)
Religion	(887)		(171)
Protestant (Percent)	52.9%	70.1%[3]	59.6%
Jewish (Percent)	13.0%	2% to 8%[4]	2.9%
Catholic (Percent)	22.5%	25.0%[3]	23.4%
Other or None	11.6%	2.9%[3]	14.1%

[1] For the general United States population. Obtained from the U.S. Bureau of the Census, *Statistical Abstract of the United States,* 106th ed., 25 and 28.

[2] These figures refer to the 1980 population of the seven districts in the main sample and are weighted to reflect the makeup of the white-collar-crime sample. Obtained from the Federal Judicial Center, *Judicial District Data Book,* 1983, and its companion computer tape (see n. 15 above). These figures have been weighted to reflect the makeup of the white-collar-crime sample.

[3] These are national figures as reported in *Public Opinion,* November–December 1978, 33.

[4] The lower figure is a national estimate from *Public Opinion,* November–December 1978, 33. The higher figure is an estimate for the Southern District of New York from Alan Chenkin, "Jewish Population in the United States, 1982," *American Jewish Yearbook,* 1983, 127–29 (see n. 28 below).

[5] These figures are calculated using only those members of the basic sample (see Appendix 1) with nonmissing values for these variables. The sample includes 1,094 individuals.

[6] These figures are calculated using only those members of the common-crime sample with nonmissing values for the variable. The sample includes 210 individuals.

men to commit crimes of great complexity and great harm, regardless of which white-collar-crime category we examine.[25] One explanation

25. See also Kathleen Daly, "Gender and Varieties of White Collar Crime," *Criminology* 27 (1989):769–93; and Lisa Maher and Elin Waring, "Beyond Simple Differences: White Collar Crime, Gender and Workforce Position," *Phoebe* 2 (1990):44–54.

for the concentration of women in these less harmful and complex crimes lies in differences in socialization of men and women in our society. Another would look to patterns of discrimination in the opportunities available to women in the workplace. In chapter 4, we will try to disentangle these two potential explanations for our findings.

The racial composition of white-collar crime is similar to that of the general population in the districts we studied. At the same time, whites as a category, like men as a category, are much more likely to be found in the upper ranges of our white-collar-crime hierarchy. This would suggest to us that there may be an element of "discrimination" in white-collar crime, as there is in the occupational structure more generally (a point we return to in more detail in the following chapter). In our common-crime sample, the percentage of nonwhites is more than twice that in our white-collar sample.

One of the most consistent findings of research on criminals is that crime is an activity of the young.[26] Our comparison group of common-crime offenders are once more atypical of the general criminal population, because they are on average older than other offenders and close to the mean age for the population as a whole. White-collar offenders are even older, with a mean age of 40. This result is not a surprising one and merely confirms a stereotype associated with white-collar criminality.

With respect to religion, one finding stands out in our data. Although those who identify themselves as Jews constitute between 2 and 8 percent of our seven-district population (and comprise only 2.9 percent of the common-crime sample), they make up 13 percent of our white-collar-crime sample. Does this finding lend any credence to the harmful stereotype of Jews as financial manipulators, or the somewhat more complex stereotype that the historical exclusion of Jews from some professions and trades and their relative disadvantage in the marketplaces of a gentile world has led to a degree of tolerance, among some Jews, for economic crimes?[27] What can our data tell us about this stereotype, or can they even begin to address it?

It is impossible for us to examine this question directly for two

26. The mean age of offenders in the criminal justice system is twenty-seven. See U.S. Department of Justice, *Uniform Crime Reports for the United States, 1977,* 180–81.

27. One case study, for example, shows how religious values can coexist with fraudulent financial activities. See Gandossy, *Bad Business.*

reasons. First, we do not know the distribution of persons in white-collar jobs by religion. It would hardly be surprising if Jews were overrepresented in white-collar crime if they more frequently hold white-collar positions, and there is every reason to believe that they do.[28] Second, we know little about the earlier stages of investigation and prosecution and about whether Jews have been discriminated against by prosecutors or others in law enforcement.

We can add a modest amount of data to the discussion by examining the distribution of Jewish offenders across the hierarchy of offenses that we introduced in chapter 2. Among those whose religion is known, the percentage of Jews rises from 9 percent in the lowest category (including bank embezzlement, tax fraud, and credit fraud) to 15 percent in the moderate category (mail fraud, false claims, and bribery) to 33 percent in the high category (antitrust and securities fraud). Although this shows a systematic progression as one works up toward the top of the hierarchy, it again may simply reflect the differential distribution of Jews in the settings that enable more sophisticated financial crimes. In our sample, for example, Jews are far more likely to be found in the securities industry than any other religious group. Of the 883 offenders whose religious preferences are known, only 10.6 percent are in finance. For Protestants, the figure is 8.8 percent, and for Catholics 7 percent. But for Jews, it is 23.9 percent. This makes their greater frequency at the top of our hierarchy understandable.[29]

28. It has been asserted that 53 percent of all employed Jewish men work in "business or the professions," as compared to 27 percent of the general employed population. The estimate of the Jewish population of New York City was obtained from data presented in the article "Jewish Population in the United States, 1982" by Alan Chenkin in the *American Jewish Yearbook, 1983* (New York: American Jewish Committee, 1982), 127–29. The estimates of Jews and the general population engaged in business and professional work (in the year 1979) come from the *American Jewish Yearbook, 1983,* 124. We attempted to find data that would tell us the distribution of specific religious groups within specific jobs during the period in question, but none were available.

29. Within the top category, 34.9 percent of the securities fraud offenders are Jewish, and 26.7 percent of the antitrust offenders are Jewish. The antitrust figure, in particular, is likely to vary from year to year, depending on the choice of target industries by the Antitrust Division of the Justice Department.

Finally, we also compared the percentage of Jews among common criminals and white-collar criminals in the three major financial centers in our sample (New York, Chicago, and Los Angeles) with their percentages in the other four cities (Atlanta, Baltimore, Dallas, and Seattle). Jews constitute 3.1 percent of the common criminals in the major cities and 2.8 percent in the others, hardly a meaningful difference. But they comprise 21.8 percent of the white-collar sample in the major cities, and only 5.1 percent in the other four.

We leave it to others to examine the relationship between religion and white-collar crime more closely. But we believe that much more needs to be learned about the distribution of various religious groups within white-collar crime and white-collar occupations before further speculation on the relationship between cultural or religious norms and white-collar criminality.

Whatever else may be true of the distinction between white-collar and common criminals, the two are definitely drawn from distinctively different sectors of the American population. While there is substantial diversity in the types of people that are found in white-collar crime, even the lowest end of our offender hierarchy is easily distinguished from offenders in common-crime categories. Some of our offenders fit the image of respectability and high social status that dominates much work on white-collar crime, but once again we are struck by the extent to which most of them fit portraits of the middle classes. They appear to represent the very broad middle of the society, much above the poverty line but for the most part far from elite social status. Like the offenses they commit, the offenders are mostly commonplace, not unlike the average American in most respects, though perhaps more often with personal lives that are in some state of disarray. The single quality that most distinguishes them from other Americans is that they have been convicted of a federal crime.

4

Opportunity in White-Collar Crime

In previous chapters our aim was to provide a detailed picture of the crimes and criminals in our sample. Aside from noting the rough hierarchies of offenses and offenders, we focused more on detail than on generalization. In this chapter our aim is different. We want to step back from these descriptions to see if we can explain critical features of white-collar crime in ways that cut across the details of individual crime categories. We are particularly interested in understanding the ways in which special opportunities available to certain offenders allow them to commit the most serious crimes. The study of common criminals has begun increasingly to focus upon characteristics of physical environments that make such crimes possible.[1] As suggested in chapter 3, we believe that the location of offenders in organizational rather than physical space is crucial for understanding white-collar crimes.

1. For example, see Paul L. Brantingham and Patricia J. Brantingham, *Environmental Criminology* (Beverly Hills, Calif.: Sage, 1981); D. C. Duffala, "Convenience Stores, Armed Robbery and Physical Environmental Features," *American Behavioral Scientist* 20 (1976):227–46; Marcus Felson, "Predicting Crime Potential at Any Point on the City Map," 127–36 in Robert M. Figlio, S. Hakim, and George F. Rengert, eds., *Metropolitan Crime Patterns* (New York: Willow Tree, 1986).

To assess the impact of white-collar crimes we found it necessary to use measures of victimization or crime seriousness that are different than those employed in the study of common crime. The use of physical violence is often seen as the most important indicator of the seriousness of street crimes.[2] And while a number of recent corporate offenses have resulted in physical harms to the public, none of our offenses (at least as described in the PSIS) involve violence in their commission. Thus, we could not rely on the use of weapons or force or on evidence of physical injury to distinguish between less and more serious white-collar crimes.

Three measures introduced in chapter 2 do allow us to differentiate the extent of victimization in our white-collar-crime cases. The first, the magnitude of the illegality, is simply the amount of money that was stolen by offenders. The large economic toll of white-collar offenses has been in great part responsible for scholarly and public interest in them. The number of victims also identifies an important dimension of the impact of such crimes. Finally, a related measure of the magnitude of white-collar crimes is their geographic spread. While common criminals generally operate in small geographic areas, most often within a few blocks from their homes,[3] as we saw in chapter 2 many white-collar crimes affect victims across different communities and often across state boundaries.

We believe that together these three measures allow us to distinguish fairly clearly between white-collar crimes with less and those with more serious impacts. We considered analyzing them separately, but statistical analyses showed a very high correlation between the three measures, and thus it would be redundant as well as unwieldy to examine them independently.[4] Moreover, we believe that the combination of these aspects of victimization, and not each alone, provides the most accurate view of the impacts of these crimes. To create the composite measure we standardized each of the measures of victimization and then summed the three standardized scores.[5]

2. See, for example, Marvin E. Wolfgang, Robert M. Figlio, Paul E. Tracy, and Simon I. Singer, *National Survey of Crime Severity* (Washington, D.C.: GPO, 1985).

3. Paul Brantingham and Patricia Brantingham, *Patterns in Crime* (New York: Macmillan, 1984), 344.

4. The Cronbach's alpha reliability score for the index developed from these measures is 0.684.

5. For the measurement of the individual variables see notes 20 and 21,

Modeling Opportunity Structures

Prior work on white-collar crime suggests several factors that influence the seriousness of the crimes that offenders commit. For example, Sutherland thought that social status was a primary factor in facilitating white-collar crime, and more recently John Hagan and Patricia Parker have looked to class position to explain the differential opportunities available to white-collar offenders.[6] In the following pages we identify a number of explanations that may be used to understand opportunity structures in white-collar crime and then test them in the context of a multivariate statistical model.

The Organizational Weapon

Complex organizations have become the essential social form in modern society, but only recently have scholars come to understand the influence of such organizations upon forms of criminal conduct. In the Yale studies of white-collar crime this concern has played a particularly important role. As Wheeler and Rothman argue:

> What difference does it make when a white-collar crime is committed in the course of one's occupation or when acting on behalf, or with the assistance, of an organization? If we are becoming, as some have argued, an organizational society, then we should see the results of this change reflected in illicit as well as licit behavior. The organizational form may be used for either social or anti-social ends. . . . [T]he organization, size and profitability notwithstanding, is for white-collar criminals what the gun or knife is for the common criminal—a tool to obtain money from victims.[7]

In chapter 3 we noted that our readings of the presentence investigations suggest that those able to use an organizational form are

---

chapter 2. The measures were converted to standardized "z-scores" (with a mean of 0 and standard deviation of 1), so that each measure would contribute more equally to the overall index, and then summed.

6. Edwin H. Sutherland, *White Collar Crime: The Uncut Version* (New Haven: Yale University Press, 1983), 3–7, 251–52, 264; and John Hagan and Patricia Parker, "White-Collar Crime and Punishment: The Class Structure and Legal Sanctioning of Securities Violations," *American Sociological Review* 50 (1985):302–16.

7. Stanton Wheeler and Mitchell Rothman, "The Organization as Weapon in White Collar Crime," *Michigan Law Review* 80 (1982):1403–26.

the criminals who appear to commit the most serious white-collar crimes. But in our view, the advantage provided by formal organization is only one part of a larger advantage that comes to those whose crimes involve greater organizational complexity. In addition to the use of the organizational form itself, those crimes that include large numbers of conspirators or which are planned and carried out over long periods of time also have an organizational edge over less complex crimes. In assessing the organizational complexity of white-collar crimes we combine four highly correlated dimensions discussed in detail in chapter 3: the duration of the offense, the number of people participating in it, whether it involved a pattern of criminal activity, and the degree of formal organization present in a conspiracy.[8]

Status, Class, and Other Indicators of a Defendant's Position and Prior Conduct

Sociologists have spent a great deal of effort in understanding the nature of social stratification—the sorting of people into hierarchical positions on the basis of their status, their class, or other social attributes. Indeed, class, status, and the closely related concepts of prestige and hierarchy are perhaps the most often studied features of social life. What was pioneering about Sutherland's introduction of the concept of white-collar crime was not the status element itself, but its introduction to a field that had assumed that there was little variation in the statuses of those ("criminals") who were studied.

The subtleties of the distinctions between status and class were beginning to be made in Sutherland's day, and they have developed greatly since then. If one were to stress the status element of social position or the ways in which those who hold certain jobs are perceived and ranked in society, the most likely measure chosen would be the Duncan Socioeconomic Index, which we introduced in chapter 3. As noted there, this measure uses the prestige, income, and educa-

8. These variables were recoded from their original forms to ranges of three or four values, and the results were summed. In the case of the presence or absence of a pattern, missing values were assigned a middle score between those for patterned and nonpatterned crimes. Individuals with missing values on the other items were coded as missing on the scale. The Cronbach's alpha for this scale is 0.70.

tional requirements associated with particular jobs to rank the status of the individuals who hold them.[9]

Scholars today distinguish social status sharply from social class. The latter concept focuses upon the power and authority that particular classes have in the workplace, rather than on the prestige associated with diverse occupations. Whether one owns a factory, or manages it, or merely works within it, for example, might be taken as a more crucial indicator of position in the social order than might the prestige or status associated with particular occupations. Indeed, some scholars have recently argued that class position, rather than social status, should occupy the center stage in studies of white-collar crime.[10] For them, it is the authority over resources and people that provides the opportunities for committing the most serious white-collar crimes. In any case, though status and class are clearly related,[11] we are convinced that they each have distinctive components, and thus we examine their effects independently.

A third indicator of social position relates to the location of offenders in the larger industrial structure of society. The type of industry in which people labor may enhance or constrain their capacity to engage in well-organized white-collar crimes with high levels of victimization. Financial markets are a key, of course, to the commission of insider trading and related crimes. On the other hand, employment in agriculture may allow few opportunities for white-collar crime or may limit work-related crimes to frauds committed against federally funded agricultural assistance programs. Position in the industrial structure has not played a central role in explanations of

9. Because a number of the criminals we studied were unemployed they received no SEI score. In order to include these people in the regression analyses presented later we randomly allocated individual scores based on the overall distribution of scores in the sample (i.e., the mean and standard deviation of the distribution did not change as a result of this process). This procedure prevents a major loss of sample cases for the analyses while randomizing systematic error.

10. Hagan and Parker, "White-Collar Crime and Punishment." See also Gilbert Geis, *On White-Collar Crime* (Lexington, Mass.: Lexington Books, 1982).

11. See David Weisburd, Elin Waring, and Stanton Wheeler, "Class, Status and the Punishment of White Collar Criminals," *Law and Social Inquiry* 50, no. 2 (1990):223–43.

white-collar crime to date, but we believe that it is a relevant dimension of white-collar criminal opportunity.

Familiar demographic items such as age, race, sex, and religious affiliation relate to the offender's position at birth or during early socialization and are, of course, basic to analyses of discrimination in all parts of American society. Failure to explore them in any inquiry risks missing important insights. We add to this group of background items "geographic location" because certain areas of the country have greater concentrations of business and financial institutions and may provide greater opportunities for commission of the most consequential white-collar crimes. Although all of our sample jurisdictions would be considered metropolitan areas, we distinguish the major financial centers of New York, Chicago, and Los Angeles from the others.

We also investigate two measures of each offender's personal history: prior criminal record; and a composite of his or her respectability as reflected by stability in marital status, employment, and residence.[12] As we noted in chapter 3, white-collar criminals frequently present an image of respectability and an unblemished record to their victims, and they may use these impressions to gain a victim's confidence.

Finally, we examine the nature of the victim in a crime as a factor that helps explain how serious are the crime's consequences. Some offenders take from individuals, others from organizations; among the latter, some steal from private businesses and others from government agencies. Some may victimize a combination of these. The choice of victim may influence how the crime is carried out and the amount of potential illegal gain.

---

12. The three measures were (1) employment stability, coded as +1 if the offender was steadily employed over the last five years; 0 if the individual was a housewife, retired, or in school; and −1 if the defendant was unemployed for large periods; (2) home ownership, coded as +1 if the defendant owned his or her own home; 0 if they rented or were in the military; and −1 if they were in an institution or homeless; (3) and marital status, coded +1 if the defendant was married for more than five years. While the Cronbach's alpha for this scale in the restricted seven district sample is only 0.57, in the larger sample (which includes additional SEC and antitrust offenders and was the basis for the construction of this index) the Cronbach's alpha is 0.80.

Who Commits the Most Serious Crimes?

In table 4.1 we show how we measured the explanatory variables just described, and table 4.2 indicates the strength of their relationships to the extent of white-collar-crime victimization.[13] As we anticipated, by far the single strongest predictor of victimization is the degree of organizational complexity used to commit the crime. Because of the central importance of this variable we will not extend our discussion of this finding here. Rather, after we have reviewed the influences of other factors on victimization, we will try to explain why some offenders are better situated to use the organizational weapon.

Of the two variables describing an offender's position in the work force—social class and industry—only the former is significant in predicting the amount of victimization caused by a crime.[14] Sole proprietors and workers commit crimes with the least impact, whereas officers and managers commit those inflicting the most harm. At first glance it may seem surprising that owners are found in the middle rather than on top of this hierarchy. This result may be confounded by the relation of ownership to the size of the organization involved in a crime. As we noted in chapter 2, our owners generally run small businesses.[15] We believe it is the power to make decisions within organizations that allows officers and managers to commit the most serious white-collar crimes. The opportunities of sole proprietors and owners (who also have such decision-making authority) are likely to be constrained by the relatively small size of the companies they control.

Though the industry in which a white-collar criminal works does not have a significant overall influence upon the degree of victimization, we find that those employed in the securities industry (including insurance) and the service sector commit crimes of significantly greater impact than those employed by the government. The place-

13. For this analysis, as well as that reported in table 4.3, we use only the seven-district sample.

14. We distinguish between individual comparisons among the categories of a variable and the significance of the variable overall.

15. The size of the organization or its resources were not systematically included in the PSIs and were thus not included in our white-collar-crime data base. Nonetheless, we were able to get a general sense of these relationships from our qualitative review of the cases.

Table 4.1. Independent Variables Used in the Analysis

Organizational Complexity[1]	A scale ranging from 4 to 13 describing the level of organizational complexity of an offense
Type of Victim	A five-category variable describing the victim of the crime
Socioeconomic Status	Duncan's Socioeconomic Index. Missing values randomly allocated
Class	A five-category variable describing the social class of the offender
Industry	A seven-category variable describing the industry in which the offender is employed during the offense
Criminal Record	A three-category variable describing the criminal history of the offender
Respectability	An index based on length of residence, marital status, and employment history. Higher scores indicate greater respectability
Education	Years of education
Sex	Female = 1, Male = 0
Race	Nonwhite = 1, White = 0
Age	Years of age
Religion	A five-category variable describing the offender's self-reported religion
District	Major financial center = 1, Other districts = 0

[1]Details on the distributions of these variables may be found in chapters 1 through 3 and in earlier sections of this chapter.

ment of the securities industry far above others supports our earlier contention that those in positions close to centers of money and power have the opportunity to commit the most consequential white-collar crimes.

There is no indication here that those who hold jobs of higher social standing are provided with a direct benefit, when we take into account the other measures we have identified. Does this mean that status is unimportant in white-collar crime? Clearly, status has an important impact on the positions offenders may gain within organi-

Table 4.2. Regression Analysis of the Victimization Caused by
Offenses

Independent Variables	Coefficient	Standardized Coefficient
Intercept	−2.157**	
Organizational Complexity	0.388***	0.429
Type of Victim[1]	***	
Government	−1.246*	−0.229
Individuals	0.138	0.014
Combination	0.847	0.110
Missing/None	−1.750***	−0.213
(Business)		
Work Force Position		
Socioeconomic Status Duncan Score	0.003	0.025
Class[1]	**	
Owner	−0.271	−0.051
Sole Proprietor	−0.676**	−0.088
Manager	−0.062	−0.008
Worker	−0.486**	−0.107
(Officer)		
Industry[1]		
Banking	0.363	0.066
Finance	0.705**	0.100
Service Sector	0.560*	0.064
Government	0.094	0.009
Production	0.418	0.086
Unemployed	0.335	0.055
(Professional Services)		
Personal History		
Criminal Record[1]	***	
Prior White-Collar Crime	0.563**	0.082
Prior Other Crime	−0.127	−0.026
(No Prior Record)		
Respectability	−0.067	−0.039
Education	0.096*	0.057
Demographic Background		
Sex	−0.131	−0.022
Race	−0.498***	−0.090
Age	−0.009	−0.048
Religion[1]		
Protestant	0.261	0.057
Jewish	−0.128	−0.017

Table 4.2. *Continued*

Independent Variables	Coefficient	Standardized Coefficient
Other Religion	0.178	0.023
None Reported	0.013	0.002
(Catholic)		
District	−0.013	0.003
Number of Cases[2]	1049	
R squared	.440	
*p < 0.05 **p < 0.01 ***p < 0.001		

[1]For variables which are represented in the equation by a set of dummy variables, the excluded category is given in parentheses. The overall significance of these variables is given opposite the variable name, while the significance of each dummy variable in relationship to the excluded category is reported next to its coefficient.

[2]This analysis uses only the individuals in the basic sample. See Appendix 1.

zations. Moreover, as will be apparent later in the chapter, status plays a role in explaining the degree of organizational complexity involved in a crime.

When we turn to the demographic measures of position—age, sex, race, religion, and geographic location—we find that only race bears a statistically significant relationship to the amount of victimization. White-collar crimes committed by whites cause more harm than those committed by nonwhites. Even if such factors as class, status, and criminal record and the degree of organization of the crime are identical for two white-collar criminals, the one who is white will generally commit a more harmful crime than the one who is not. Although our data do not give us any information about how this "discrimination" operates, this finding will come as no surprise to many. As one prominent black New York politician noted during a municipal bribery scandal: "Hell no, you're not going to see any blacks of consequence indicted in this corruption scandal. We never got invited to the table when the pie was being divided up. We didn't even know there was a pie. . . . Candidly, [the mayor] didn't even give us an equal opportunity to steal."[16]

16. Quoted in Andy Logan, "Around City Hall," *New Yorker,* September 14, 1987, 126.

Our finding that there is not a significant difference between the harms inflicted by men and women contradicts a widely held view that women, even when in similar positions to men, are less prone to carry out serious illegalities. It is something of a rarity in our sample, as in society generally, for women to occupy the highest status positions or to commit crimes with very serious victimization. But we do have examples of such cases. For instance, one woman was an executive vice president of a real estate company and was a central participant in one of the largest frauds in the sample. Our results suggest that if more women enter such powerful positions their crimes will be very similar in their impact to those of men. Returning to a question we raised in chapter 3, we believe that the structural positions of women, not socialization processes, account for the gender differences in victimization in our sample.[17]

Of the characteristics describing the personal histories of offenders, prior criminal record and education have statistically significant influences upon victimization. The much larger effect is that of prior record, though better-educated offenders seem to have a marginal advantage in white-collar crime. Those with prior white-collar criminal convictions, on average, commit the most consequential white-collar crimes, while those with common-crime records have even lower levels of victimization than those without any criminal record. It has long been argued that the pariah status of criminality does not pass to those convicted of white-collar crimes,[18] and our results support this contention, at least as regards potential for future white-collar criminality. Those with only prior white-collar crime records, in contrast to those who have committed any common crimes, are not denied opportunities for serious white-collar crime. Indeed, their experience seems to facilitate such offenses.

A very strong predictor of the degree of victimization is the type of victim. Those who have either the government as their victim or no identifiable victim commit crimes that rank relatively low on our

17. For another view of this problem also developed from these data, see Kathleen Daly, "Gender and Varieties of White Collar Crime," *Criminology* 27 (1989):769–93; and Lisa Maher and Elin Waring, "Beyond Simple Differences: White Collar Crimes, Gender and Workforce Position," *Phoebe* 2 (1990): 44–54.

18. Indeed, this was one of Sutherland's main contentions. See Sutherland, *White Collar Crime,* chap. 4, esp. 54–60.

victimization measure, while cases where there are multiple types of victims rank highest, and business and individual victimizations fall somewhere in between. This difference is not simply an artifact of our measure of victimization (which includes an indicator of the number of victims affected), with government agencies being low on our index because they are most likely to be one-target crimes. Even when we look at monetary damages alone, crimes against government agencies are still of lower magnitude than other white-collar crimes. Misrepresentations to HUD, briberies of tax auditors, and false claims on government employment forms seldom yield large sums of money for their perpetrators. In contrast those offenses that spread their victimization across multiple types of victims are likely to net extremely large sums of money.[19]

There is little in the literature on victimization that can help us to interpret this result, but it seems to us that the choice of victim has an important relationship to our earlier finding concerning the role of organizational complexity in white-collar crime. Virtually all citizens are in positions to steal from the government, most notably if they choose to cheat the IRS but also from their contacts with numerous other agencies that give or take money from the public. In contrast, it takes real entrepreneurship, albeit fraudulent entrepreneurship, to organize a phony land sale or to perpetrate a securities fraud. Those with entrepreneurial spirit are perhaps more likely to end up in the securities business, where there are greater opportunities to organize complex frauds. Less well-placed individuals may choose from more easily available but less richly rewarding opportunities that depend on lying to the government.

In summary, the measure of organizational complexity is the single strongest predictor of how much damage, or criminal victimization, will occur. Of indicators of social position, class is overall a significant factor for explaining victimization (with managers and officers able to carry out the most serious crimes), and those in the securities industry commit more serious crimes than those in the service sector. Strikingly, social status itself has no direct impact on victimization, though the status of minority group member serves to suppress the amount of victimization. History of prior common-

19. Of course, these analyses emphasize the average cases in some of these broad categories. As noted in chapter 3 a number of frauds against the government involve very large sums of money.

criminal conduct also reduces opportunity for victimization, though prior experience in white-collar crime increases the opportunity for victimization. Better-educated offenders also commit more costly crimes. Finally, when the government is the target, victimizations are likely to be relatively less serious, as compared with cases that involve business, individual, and multiple victims.

Although no single presentence investigation provides evidence of all of these findings, many illustrate the relationships identified in our model. For example, one offender in a major credit-fraud case was the chairman of the board of directors of a bank and also a senior partner in a financially troubled company that processed wood chips. He obtained very large bank loans that would not normally have been approved by the bank. He was also a director of another company that had the controlling interest in the bank, and in a proxy statement to its shareholders he failed to disclose the various loans his company had received. Over the years in which these operations took place, the estimated loss to the bank was almost $6 million. Clearly, the chairman's class position made such a dramatic crime possible.

In another case, the chief partner in a brokerage firm that handled the purchase and sale of large blocks of stock for financial institutions worked out a kickback plan with a securities trader for one of the banks. The trader would receive a portion of the brokerage firm's profits for the bank's transactions. As the relationship evolved, the coconspirator employed by the bank agreed to a plan whereby he would buy and sell stocks in a way that artificially increased their prices, thereby creating more profit for the firm at the expense of the bank's investors. This scheme took place over a three-to-four-year period, netting a total profit estimated at some $10 million. Here we see the usefulness of employment in a position of authority in the financial industry, and the benefits of organizationally complex schemes involving a number of conspirators acting in concert over a long period. This crime also benefited from the targeting of a combination of organizational and individual victims.

The importance of "organization," as opposed to legitimate formal organizational structures, is illustrated in a number of cases where organizations are established specifically to commit crimes. In one such case, for example, the offender created a company of which he became president, chairman of the board, and a major stock holder. He used the company to solicit funds to purchase undeveloped land.

He created a number of shell companies, which he directed as a front for his scheme. Over a four-year period approximately three hundred investors contributed in excess of $5 million.

Opportunity and Organizational Complexity

Given the critical role of organization and its related variables, we turn now to an effort to understand how our various measures of offender position, history, and background relate to organizational complexity. Our analysis proceeds along the same lines as that used for victimization with two exceptions. First, the index of organizational complexity itself is, of course, removed from the list of predictor variables, because it is what we are trying to predict. Second, the relationship between social status and organizational complexity is treated as nonlinear and is represented by two variables in table 4.3.[20]

Before turning to an examination of particular relationships, we want to note two overall differences between the results reported in table 4.2 and those in table 4.3. First, we do a slightly better job of explaining victimization than organizational complexity. The proportion of variance explained for victimization is 0.44, whereas that for organizational complexity is 0.36. Second, though the percent of variance explained is smaller, we find a larger number of our predictors have significant influences (see table 4.3). In particular, it appears, as we will detail below, that measures of status and respectability, which do not play a role in explaining victimization, do help to explain why some people rather than others are in positions to commit crimes of greater organizational complexity. Now let us examine, as before, each of the separate domains we identify.

All three measures of position in the work force show significant relationships. Industry is significant overall, with those in the securities industry again committing the most complex offenses. At the opposite end of the spectrum is the banking industry, whose employees commit less complex crimes than even the unemployed. This appears to contradict our contention that those in positions close to

20. Our decision to use a polynomial trend to describe the influence of status developed from review of bivariate scatterplots for independent variables in the model.

Table 4.3. Regression Analysis of the Organizational Complexity of Offenses

Independent Variables	Coefficient	Standardized Coefficient
Intercept	7.479***	
Type of Victim[1]	***	
Government	−1.876**	−0.312
Individuals	−0.208	−0.020
Combination	−0.373	−0.044
Missing/None	−0.827	−0.091
(Business)		
Work Force Position	*	
Socioeconomic Status Duncan Score	0.033*	0.252
Duncan Score Squared	−0.0003*	−0.261
Class[1]	***	
Owner	−0.608*	−0.104
Sole Proprietor	−1.187***	−0.141
Manager	0.102	0.012
Worker	−0.853***	−0.170
(Officer)		
Industry[1]	***	
Banking	−1.302***	−0.209
Finance	0.604*	0.077
Service Sector	−0.024	−0.002
Government	0.306	0.026
Manufacturing	−0.052	−0.010
Unemployed	−0.965**	−0.142
(Professional Services)		
Personal History		
Criminal Record[1]		
Prior White-Collar Crime	−0.020	−0.003
Prior Other Crime	−0.023	−0.004
(No Prior Record)		
Respectability	0.201**	0.106
Education	0.150**	0.080
Demographic Background		
Sex	−0.025	−0.004
Race	−0.203	−0.034
Age	0.029***	0.136
Religion[1]		
Protestant	0.016	0.003
Jewish	0.481	0.059
Other Religion	0.363	0.042

Table 4.3. *Continued*

Independent Variables	Coefficient	Standardized Coefficient
None Reported (Catholic)	0.222	0.034
District	0.653***	0.131
Number of Cases[2]	1049	
R squared	0.359	
*p < 0.05 **p < 0.01 ***p < 0.001		

[1] For variables which are represented in the equation by a set of dummy variables, the excluded category is given in parentheses. The overall significance of these variables is given opposite the variable name, while the significance of each dummy variable in relationship to the excluded category is reported next to its coefficient.

[2] This analysis uses only the individuals in the basic sample. See Appendix 1.

money and power are advantaged in white-collar crime. But it should be noted that the banking industry, as contrasted, for example, with securities firms, is subject to intense and frequent auditing, ranging from end-of-the-day counting of cash in tellers' drawers to the monitoring done by the Federal Deposit Insurance Corporation (FDIC), Federal Savings and Loan Insurance Corporation (FSLIC), and Federal Reserve. Such regulation may, all else being equal, make banking institutions places where more organizationally complex crimes are harder to develop. Our cases, of course, are drawn from the period before deregulation of the savings and loan industry.

The influence of social class is similar to that found in the prior analysis, with sole proprietors and workers significantly less well positioned than managers or corporate officers. Again, a managerially powerful position tends to facilitate the commission of organizationally complex crimes.

The third measure of work-force position, socioeconomic status, also significantly influences organizational complexity, though it bore no relationship to victimization. This relationship is not linear, as illustrated in figure 4.1. Those of moderate rather than high social status commit the most highly organized white-collar offenses and thus the ones that yield the greatest payoffs. Here, status benefits

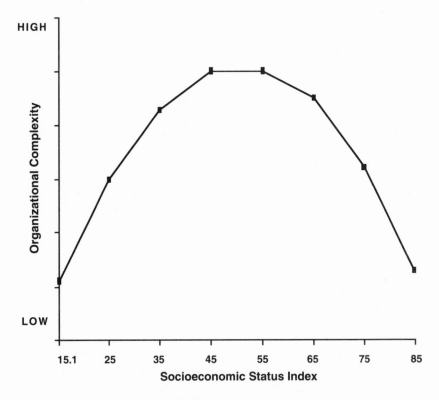

Figure 4.1. Relationship between Social Status and Organizational Complexity

those of moderate social stature, such as managers or bookkeepers, but not those who, like lawyers and doctors, occupy the highest status positions. How can we explain this surprising finding?

We speculate that the individualism and independence encouraged by professional norms discourage the highest status offenders from developing highly organized criminal behavior by encouraging individual initiative more than organizational cooperation.[21] How-

21. Our findings may reflect as well the fact that professionals are not generally in powerful positions in the large organizational contexts that facilitate white-collar offending. Our class variable may capture some but not all of this relationship.

ever, the growing participation of professionals in large private organizations rather than small partnerships may lead to changes in both their opportunities for and attitudes toward complex white-collar criminality. For example, we know from the PSIS that when doctors organize Medicaid clinics in order to loot the government their crimes can be complex and profitable.

Our findings also reflect the fact that those in the highest status positions often do not use their positions as a means of committing their crimes. Some of the simplest tax crimes are committed by physicians, lawyers, and ministers. High occupational status may offer many advantages in this world, but it appears to be neither a guarantee against becoming a criminal nor an assurance that one's crimes will be organizationally complex.

Our demographic background measures—age, sex, race, religion, and geographic location—bear interesting transformations in their relationship to complexity, as compared to victimization. In the prior model, only race was directly related to victimization. In this case, the significant effect of race disappears (though the trend remains in the same direction), and age becomes highly significant. Religion, as before, has no overall effect. Gender remains insignificant, but geographic location becomes a significant factor, with those in districts that include larger financial centers committing the most complex crimes. How can we account for these changes in effects?

Differences in the roles of age and geographic location are perhaps easiest to disentangle. Age itself does not help to develop crimes of more serious impact. But with age come special opportunities to develop social networks within organizations over long periods of time. Trust that develops between business associates, or those in business and their customers, not only lends credibility to misrepresentations but also facilitates the development of complex offenses. Many of the securities and antitrust crimes we examined, for example, involve several offenders who have long-term business relationships. Such bonds both enable the commission of such crimes and aid in their cover-up and hence in their delayed discovery.

Districts in major economic centers provide the opportunity for offenses involving greater organizational complexity, just as they provide greater opportunity for more complex conventional economic activity. That this relationship is strong even though we are making comparisons among seven urban areas, all of which are relatively cosmopolitan, is telling. Presumably, we might have found even greater differences had we included the smaller cities found in the vast majority of federal districts.

The changing role of race is perhaps more difficult to understand. Why should nonwhites be committing crimes with less serious victimization, but not ones that are less complex? To some degree we might suspect that the barriers of discrimination would apply not only to how much is taken but to the opportunities for developing the types of schemes that are likely to have a high yield. But precisely because racial groups are subject to exclusion they are also more likely to form strong networks within organizations, and this might lead to greater organizational complexity in their crimes. Overall, we suspect that the latter is true, but that minorities have not entered organizations in large enough numbers to achieve what Rosabeth Moss Kanter has identified as a "threshold of power."[22] A similar logic may explain the lack of a significant relation between gender and the commission of organizationally complex crimes.

Whereas in our earlier model prior record had a significant influence and our measure of respectability no significant influence, here the findings are reversed. Prior experience in white-collar crime does not help to develop crimes of greater organizational complexity, though as we saw earlier it does contribute to an offender's ability to commit offenses of greater victimization. At the same time, those with the appearance of greater respectability, either reflected in our general index or by education (which is again statistically significant), are able to commit more complex offenses. We cannot attribute these results to the fact that people who score high on respectability or education are more likely to hold statuses that provide opportunities for more complex crimes, since we control for occupational status and for class position. Rather, these attributes may provide a kind of protection by encouraging others to assume that the defendant is trustworthy and may thereby facilitate the offender's use of an organization to commit a crime.

Finally, we turn to the type of victim. Choosing businesses as the

22. See Rosabeth Moss Kanter, *Men and Women of the Corporation* (New York: Basic Books, 1977). Kanter discusses the isolation of token members of organizations (especially women) and the difficulties they face because of it, like lack of system knowledge and restricted access to sponsors, alliances with peers, awareness of benefits and perquisites, etc. See chapters 7 and 8.

target of an offense results in more complex offending, whereas victimizing the government seems to result in crimes of little organizational complexity. This may relate again to the kinds of opportunities for crime that government presents. As we noted earlier, the crimes involving government victimizations usually do not require much sophistication to carry out.

Old and New Paths to White-Collar Crime

Just as common crime opportunities are linked to physical aspects of environment, white-collar victimization is linked to an offender's place in organizational space. The authority and power associated with class position, the opportunities offered by working in certain industries or by choosing particular types of victims, all increase the offender's ability to inflict greater harm on the community. Our finding that the organizational complexity of an offense is the single most powerful predictor of victimization suggests that organization itself, rather than social position or status, should be central to the study of the consequences of white-collar crimes. It is, as Wheeler and Rothman suggest, a weapon that is primarily responsible for the transfer of goods or funds from the victim to the offender.

This latter finding enriches our understanding of white-collar crime, not only because it identifies organization as a central dimension but also because it helps us to understand the complex relationship between social standing and white-collar offending. We have already noted that our sample includes many people who do not fit the usual image of the white-collar criminal. Yet, many of these offenders commit very serious crimes. The role of organization provides us with a more subtle understanding of this process. We believe that it demands rethinking of a tradition in study of white-collar crime that identifies a direct linear relationship between social status and white-collar criminal opportunities.

The following two cases, which involved complex frauds and netted large sums of money, illustrate how organizational complexity can transcend status. The first involved two employees of one of the nation's largest consumer credit reporting agencies, which provides banks, credit card companies, and retail stores with computer printouts of credit histories. One of the offenders (A) was employed in the file room of the company and the other (B) had access to the computer used in the processing of credit histories. B convinced A that for a fee of $50 to $100 per case he should alter credit histories at B's direction. The two had many meetings during which B reviewed the credit histories of his clients and instructed A to delete certain items and to add others. B then made the corresponding changes on the computer.

In the second case, individuals affiliated with a church were able to defraud the government out of nearly a $1 million over four years. A day-care center operating through the church was supposed to provide meals and food supplements to children at the center with reimbursement from the Department of Agriculture. To receive reimbursements the offenders were required to prepare monthly vouchers indicating the total number of meals served that were eligible for reimbursement and the cost of food and labor. They consistently overstated these figures. Interviews with employees, teachers, and teachers' aides revealed that morning snacks were never served unless the government inspectors were expected, that the same children were run through serving lines twice when inspectors were present, and that some children were bused in from other day-care centers on inspection days. Several teachers reported that they prepared snacks at home and brought them in because the children were hungry and had difficulty concentrating. The apparently legitimate billings for the monthly invoices were approximately $79 thousand, though the defendant's claims totaled nearly $1 million in food costs and $400 thousand in labor.

In both of these cases, persons of modest social status were able to carry out crimes of relatively high organizational complexity, and it was that complexity rather than their social standing that allowed them to carry out crimes of great harm. In the first, the special access to computer information gave the offenders the opportunity for complex criminality, an opportunity which would not have existed when information was less easily accessed. The school-lunch scheme involved people of middle-level status in most other respects who took advantage of the opportunities for criminality that grew out of federal welfare programs. These cases suggest to us that opportunities for white-collar crime are now available to people outside the elite group that generated Sutherland's interest.

5

From Offense to Conviction

The experience of white-collar criminals as they move through the criminal justice system has drawn much contemporary interest. In part, this concern has developed from a widely held perception that criminal justice agents from police to judges treat higher status offenders more leniently than other, less privileged lawbreakers. Yet, attention has also been focused on the more punitive effects that legal processing may have on white-collar criminals. In particular, it has been assumed that they are much more likely to suffer public humiliation and loss of job or position in the community than are common-crime defendants.[1] In this chapter we describe the paths that convicted offenders take through the legal system and the impact of the legal process upon white-collar criminals and their families.

Paths through the Legal Process

Discovery of the Crime

The treatment of white-collar criminals in the legal system starts off very differently from that of common criminals in great part

1. See Stanton Wheeler, Kenneth Mann, and Austin Sarat, *Sitting in Judgment* (New Haven: Yale University Press, 1988); and Michael Levi, *Reg-*

because of differences in the way these crimes are carried out and in the nature of their victims. Many white-collar crimes go undetected for months or years; seldom does the detection take the form of a victim calling the authorities shortly after the occurrence of the crime. Indeed, some theorists of white-collar crime have argued that one of its primary definitional characteristics is that its victims are unaware that they have been victimized.[2] The long duration of many of the crimes in our sample is a reflection of this reality.[3]

How white-collar crimes are detected is thus an important issue. We find that there are three major paths that lead authorities to the crimes: evidence is provided by victims, the crime is discovered through routine government audits or investigations, or information is provided by informants. Occasionally, crimes are disclosed when an offender confesses or when a special investigation is conducted, but these events occur too rarely to single them out for separate analysis.

Of all the white-collar offenses, bank embezzlement comes closest to the patterns of discovery ordinarily encountered in street crimes:[4] three-quarters of bank embezzlements are discovered by authorities

---

ulating Fraud: White-Collar Crime and the Criminal Process (New York: Tavistock, 1987).

2. For example, see Herbert Edelhertz, *The Nature, Impact and Prosecution of White Collar Crime* (Washington, D.C.: U.S. Department of Justice, Law Enforcement Assistance Administration, National Institute of Law Enforcement and Criminal Justice, 1970).

3. Once again we caution the reader that our findings are based only on convicted defendants. Unlike the largely unknown population of white-collar criminals whose crimes are never detected, whose identities are never discovered, or who are punished administratively, all of the criminals in our sample came into contact with the criminal-justice system. Unlike others who have been formally accused of white-collar crime but acquitted, or convicted of misdemeanors, they have been convicted of felonies. Thus, their experiences as defendants cannot provide a complete picture of the experiences of white-collar criminals in the legal process. Despite this limitation, we believe that much can be gained by examining the offenders in our sample in light of these issues.

4. Our comparison common-crime sample is very similar to our bribery and antitrust groups in terms of discovery, and thus departs from this general pattern. We believe that this result (like those we discuss when examining charging later in the chapter) is linked more strongly to the limitations imposed upon us in our choice of a comparison sample than to similarities between white-collar and common crime generally. Accordingly, common-crime statistics are excluded from table 5.1.

Table 5.1. How the Offense Was Detected (for the Case Sample)

	By Victim or Offender's Employer	By Routine Audit or Investigation	By Informant	Other	N^3
Bank Embezzlement	74.8%	17.0%	4.4%	3.8%	159
Credit Fraud	58.2%	19.0%	7.6%	15.2%	84
Mail Fraud	55.9%	23.5%	11.8%	8.8%	81
Tax	4.4%	79.7%	4.4%	11.6%	143
Securities Fraud[1]	17.7%	39.3%	14.3%	28.6%	56
False Claims	23.8%	41.3%	27.5%	7.5%	82
Antitrust[1]	20.0%	20.0%	40.0%	20.0%	23
Bribery	22.0%	29.3%	34.2%	14.6%	57
All White-Collar Crimes[2]	40.4%	39.4%	11.3%	8.9%	540

[1] Includes the national samples of securities and antitrust cases.
[2] Includes the basic sample of white-collar crimes. See Appendix 2.
[3] N represents the number of individuals with nonmissing information for the variable. See Appendix 2.

when the victim (the bank or its depositors) seeks criminal prosecution (table 5.1). But in contrast to most street crimes, bank embezzlements are often discovered as a result of internal audits, including counting cash at the end of the day. Given the inclusion in this category of many relatively simple crimes that often resemble theft, the dominance of this mode of discovery is not surprising.

More than half of all credit-fraud and mail-fraud cases are also discovered by victims. Given the frequent presence of individuals as targets in these frauds, and the fact that the offenders operate in relatively unregulated environments, it may be that the authorities do not actively seek out these crimes but rather depend upon the victims to sort out honest transactions from fraudulent ones.

In contrast, where there is extensive public-agency record keeping, routine government audits and investigations yield many of the successful prosecutions. Tax fraud is the clearest example; nearly 80 percent of the cases begin with something detected in a routine audit or investigation initiated by the government. This method is also prominent in securities frauds and false-claims cases. Many of these crimes are discovered because the records of some government agency contain a paper trail that offenders could not eradicate. Often canceled checks, fraudulent tax returns, or other official forms allow prosecutors to make their cases.

Collusive crimes are distinctive in the reliance of the authorities on informants. Antitrust cases are prominent here, with more than half of them detected this way. Successful price-fixing conspiracies may victimize thousands of consumers without their ever becoming aware that a crime has been committed. While the public and law enforcement agencies may notice unduly high prices that are the result of an illegal conspiracy, successful prosecution requires specific knowledge of the telephone calls, meetings, or other activities in which the prices are illegally set. Without this, high prices could be assumed to be the result of legitimate economic forces in the marketplace, rather than the product of an illegal conspiracy. Informants are crucial to determining both that a crime occurred and who carried it out.

Bribery, like antitrust, is a crime of collusion, and in many bribery cases, the suspect is "set up" by authorities with the assistance of another party to the bribe who has turned informant. Often, law enforcement officials are informed before the actual payoff about the initial offer or request for a bribe. The government may place a "wire" or hidden microphone on the body of the informant. When the informant next meets the suspect, the bribe is recorded, and the suspect is caught in the act. In one case, five individuals, including two prison guards, sought a $25 thousand bribe in return for the successful escape of a prisoner. The prisoner informed the authorities, and the offenders were set up by the Drug Enforcement Administration and local police agents. In another case, a paid informant in an ongoing federal narcotics investigation called one of the people against whom he was supposed to offer evidence and asked for $10 thousand in return for not testifying. That person told his attorney, who notified the local prosecutor. The authorities then monitored a phone call during which the informant agreed to take $55 hundred.

These materials support Susan Shapiro's observation that the method of discovery in white-collar crime plays an important role in determining the types of offenses that come to prosecution.[5] Relying

5. Susan Shapiro, *Wayward Capitalists: Targets of the Securities and Exchange Commission* (New Haven: Yale University Press, 1984). See especially chapters 3 and 7. Chapter 7 gives evidence of the different intelligence strategies and the types of offenses they detect.

on victims in white-collar crime will lead to the discovery of a preponderance of embezzlements, and credit and mail frauds. Conspiracies, like antitrust and bribery, are less likely to be revealed without informers. Studies specifically designed to examine detection will tell us more.[6]

Choice of Counsel

In white-collar crime cases legal counsel are involved at a much earlier stage than in common crimes.[7] From the time there is even a hint that a possible white-collar crime is under investigation by legal authorities, individuals suspected of involvement often begin to retain attorneys and to prepare to defend themselves. Early legal strategies may include negotiations with the agencies involved, the seeking of civil or out-of-court resolution of the case, and the trading of information in return for favorable treatment from the prosecutor's office. Other strategies include defense efforts to limit the scope of the information sought through subpoenaed documents and to curtail the information obtained by the government through search warrants and electronic surveillance.

There is every reason to believe that the quality of legal counsel, important in any criminal case, is especially important for defendants charged with white-collar crime. Early involvement of a skilled specialist in white-collar-crime defense may stave off prosecution altogether, or failing that may bring an experienced negotiator to the table when a deal is cut with the prosecutor.

The length of this process, as well as the work of the defense counsel, is well illustrated by one of our cases. A tax evader was charged on a single count by information on February 22, 1978. He pleaded guilty to the charge on March 1, 1978 and was sentenced on April 3, 1978. His formal contacts with the criminal justice system, from charge to sentence, lasted only slightly longer than one month.

6. These materials should be treated as suggestive at best, both because we are missing information on a substantial number of cases and because it is probable that the mode of detection has some influence on the success of prosecution. It is also the case that particular policies of individual U.S. Attorney's offices may influence which modes of detection are emphasized in criminal investigations.

7. Kenneth Mann, *Defending White-Collar Crime* (New Haven: Yale University Press, 1985), 9.

However, the investigation of the tax evader actually began in September 1973, when he was first approached by the IRS. His first formal interview with the IRS was in May 1975, nearly three years prior to the filing of charges. In the beginning of 1977 he made the front page of the local newspaper with his plan to challenge the IRS probe. Thus, his actual involvement with the authorities lasted some five years.

Given the important early role played by defense attorneys in these cases, it is crucial for a suspect to hire an attorney during the preliminary stages. To wait until an indictment is to risk serious consequences. It thus comes as no surprise that the majority of white-collar criminals in our sample retain their own counsel, while only 16 percent of our common criminals are represented by private attorneys (table 5.2).[8]

If anything, what is surprising is that more than 40 percent of the white-collar criminals do not retain their own private counsel and are dependent on public defenders or court-appointed attorneys.[9] Whatever their financial condition during their criminal activities, at this stage of the legal process they could be classed as "indigent" defendants and thus qualified for public legal assistance.

The retention of private attorneys correlates highly with the hierarchy of white-collar crime we discussed in chapters 2 and 3. At the top, all of the antitrust offenders retain private counsel. At the other end of the hierarchy, only one-third of those convicted of bank embezzlement do so. This is a substantially higher figure than for our common-crime sample, but it again suggests the range and diversity of defendants convicted under white-collar-crime statutes.

8. Beyond this, research by Jonathan D. Casper (*American Criminal Justice: The Defendant's Perspective* [Englewood Cliffs, N.J.: Prentice-Hall, 1972]) documents that criminal defendants *believe* they are getting more supportive and aggressive lawyers when they have paid for their own lawyers rather than accept what the system provides. See also Elin Waring, David Weisburd, and Stanton Wheeler, "The Impact of the Type of Defense Attorney on Legal Strategies: Exploratory Observations Using a Sample of Convicted White Collar Criminals" (paper presented at the Law and Society Association Meeting, Madison, Wisconsin, June 1989).

9. In the Southern District of New York defendants are represented by the Legal Aid Society rather than by public defenders. When we refer to public defenders in the remaining sections of the chapter, legal aid representation will be included.

Table 5.2. Defendants with Privately Retained Counsel

Offense	Percent with Privately Retained Counsel	N[3]
Antitrust[1]	100.0%	54
Securities Fraud[1]	81.3%	146
Bribery	78.3%	46
Tax Fraud	61.3%	106
False Claims	57.9%	114
Credit Fraud	54.6%	108
Mail Fraud	51.4%	109
Bank Embezzlement	33.9%	121
All White-Collar Crimes[2]	56.7%	668
Common Crimes	15.7%	140

[1] Includes the national samples of securities and antitrust offenders. See Appendix 1.
[2] Includes the basic sample only. See Appendix 1.
[3] N represents the number of individuals with nonmissing information for the variable. See Appendix 1.

Undoubtedly, the single most important factor that distinguishes those with privately retained counsel from the others is access to money. As our earlier analysis showed, credit-fraud and false-claims offenders are less well off financially than SEC offenders, so it is not surprising that fewer than two-thirds of the former, compared to four-fifths of the latter, retain private counsel.

What is less evident is why substantial minorities of the securities-fraud, bribery, and tax offenders do not retain private counsel. A close look at the offenders suggests the nature of their apparent financial problems. Even multimillion dollar schemes often do not leave defendants with enough ready cash or unmortgaged property to retain their own lawyers. For example, a securities violator in the Southern District of New York, who had been the president of a brokerage firm and a member of the New York State Bar, was represented by a court-appointed attorney. He reported that, during the nine-month period in which the offense was committed, his first wife was in the hospital dying of cancer, and the brokerage firm was in dire financial straits. He claimed that he did not benefit personally from the securities violation but put the money back into the firm for operating capital. In his interview with the probation officer preparing his presentence investigation report, the securities violator reported liabilities of more than $534 thousand and no assets.

Financial need resulting in part from alcoholism or other addictions is present in a small number of cases, and often explains the lack of private counsel. One offender in the Chicago metropolitan area, for example, who was convicted of five counts of failure to file income-tax returns, had worked for a family-owned advertising and art business after leaving the Marine Corps. The tax evader, an alcoholic and the son of an alcoholic father, had invested in a new home shortly before his wife sued for divorce. As a result of his alcoholism, he had not held a steady job in the two years before his arrest, and he had no apparent funds. He was represented by an attorney from the federal public defender's office.

As these cases demonstrate, a white-collar job and a middle-class background are no assurance of financial security, and the vast majority of the offenders who do not hire private counsel do not have the money to do so. But there is another small category whose motivations are more complex. In these cases, defendants waive their right to counsel in order to create an impression of remorse or to make a political statement, although the nature of their motives varies greatly, as the following two cases illustrate.

Both cases come from the Northern District of Texas, although there the similarity ends. In the first, a fifty-seven-year-old man, married since 1945, who had worked all of his adult life as a building contractor, was charged with bribing a contract officer for the Army and Air Force Exchange Services. He had suffered business reversals, had declared bankruptcy a year or two earlier, and was desperately trying to bail himself out. As a respected churchgoer with an impressive military record, the defendant advised the judge that although he could afford an attorney he desired to enter his plea without legal representation. In a written statement he said:

> There are several reasons for my remorse. First, I was a person who had never broken the law; I was a person who loved, fought, and was injured for America, and its form of law and order. I was the type person that people respected and admired. Second, and the one that perhaps hurts the most, is the feeling that I betrayed

the trust of my family. My wife of 32 years and 4 children have always looked to me for Christian guidance and principles. I have always tried to set a good example. I am proud of my family and love them very much. . . . I appreciate this opportunity to put into writing some of the actions, involvements and feelings which are connected to this case. I have always been a productive citizen and hope by your kindness and the grace of God to continue in that capacity.

This offender, despite his financial setbacks, still had managed to retain his own home and probably could have gotten further financial help from family and friends to hire a private attorney. But since he was prepared not only to admit his guilt but to confess publicly, he apparently saw a benefit to speaking directly to the court about his case, and no real need for private counsel.

The second case involved an IRS offense, submitting a false W–4E form to an employer. The offender also represented himself and made the following statement:

> In 1975 I was told that the government was spending a big portion of our tax money for things that didn't help the American people. I started researching this situation and found it to be true resulting from the information I could find. Also the H.E.W. Dept. was funding abortions through Medicaid at $50 million dollars a year. I didn't like what I found, and I was told that I could legally stop my tax support of these things by filing what is known as a Fifth Amendment Income Tax Packet including a Redress of Grievances. . . .
>
> . . . If enough people did this the government would have to change the way they are wasting our tax money and start using this money for the good of the American public. This is what I was trying to do and by filing the W–4E with my employer I violated Section 7205 because of the I.R.S. interpretation of a liability which is different from what I thought a liability was.
>
> Now I feel that what I was trying to do is still right, but I went about it the wrong way. What I need to do is try to get the changes made through legislation.

This defendant is typical of the tax protestors in our sample. In this case, his protest netted him a nine-month sentence, of which he was

Table 5.3. Cooperation with Authorities

	Percent Cooperating with Authorities	N^3
Securities Fraud[1]	20.0%	225
Bribery	14.3%	84
Mail Fraud	8.4%	190
False Claims	5.1%	157
Credit Fraud	10.8%	158
Antitrust[1]	8.5%	117
Tax Fraud	3.3%	210
Bank Embezzlement	3.0%	201
All White-Collar Crimes[2]	7.7%	1,090
Common Crimes	11.9%	210

[1] Includes the national samples of securities and antitrust offenders. See Appendix 1.

[2] Includes the basic sample only. See Appendix 1.

[3] N represents the number of individuals with nonmissing information for the variable. See Appendix 1.

to serve thirty days, with the remainder on probation, and a $500 fine.

The Role of Cooperating Defendants

One of the earliest decisions a defendant can make is whether or not to cooperate with the authorities by providing information that may lead to charges against others. The widespread use of informants in the discovery of a number of our crimes had led us to expect that more of our white-collar criminals would cooperate in this way than is indicated in table 5.3, and it is quite likely that there are many cases of cooperation that are not evident in the PSIs. In any event, only 8 percent of our white-collar criminals are noted to have cooperated with prosecutors. Even for crime categories in which informants are often used to discover an offense, such as antitrust and bribery, relatively few offenders provide information.[10] Our common

10. This would imply either that informants were often not involved in the crimes or that prosecutors were less likely to bring criminal charges against informants than against those who were informed upon.

Table 5.4. Cooperation by Role in the Offense for White-Collar
Criminals[1]

Role in Offense	Percent Cooperating with Authorities	N
Acted Alone	1.3%	554
Acted in a Group of Equals	8.0%	100
In Offenses with Differentiated Roles		
Central Role	6.5%	153
Middle Role	15.0%	40
Minor Role	24.4%	126

[1] Includes the basic sample only. See Appendix 1.

criminals are roughly similar in the percentage who cooperate,
though here, too, we expect underreporting.

It is common wisdom among many in the white-collar crime bar
that law-enforcement officials want to be selective in whom they use
as informants, although they often take whom they can get. Key
players will be the least likely to be sought as informers, because they
are the most culpable defendants and thus should get the harshest
punishments. Valuable information is likely to be forthcoming only if
the defendant can benefit, for example, by a reduction in the number
or severity of charges. Prosecutors, for whom success may be measured by the severity of sentences imposed in their cases, are therefore unlikely to give up their chances for stiff sanctions by trading for
information with these central figures. Rather, "little fish" who can
deliver the "big fish" are prime targets for information seeking.

This common wisdom is confirmed in our data (table 5.4). Whereas
only 7 percent of the primary players (in offenses with multiple levels)
supply information, 15 percent of those in the middle and a quarter of
those who play the least important roles in these crimes cooperate
with the government. While those lower down in schemes are clearly
much more likely to provide information, it might be asked why we
find a fairly substantial number of "big fish" who also do. Our readings
of the PSIS suggest that schemes are often so large and sophisticated
that a prosecutor needs the help of a primary player if a major case is
to be won. Of course, sometimes who is "big" and who is "little" can
only be discerned after the fact, and in the rush to the prosecutor's

office the key players also have the most information to offer. This is one reason why financial entrepreneurs like Dennis Levine and Ivan Boesky cooperated with prosecutors despite playing central roles in their crimes.[11]

The Charging Decision

Once a crime is detected and a decision to prosecute is made, the next formal step is the filing of charges (although the specific charges may be amended at a later time). The process leading up to the filing of charges is of great importance because the formal charge determines the degree of exposure to various sanctions at time of sentencing. The delicate process of negotiation between prosecutors and experienced defense counsel (who themselves are often former prosecutors) is well known to the participants but is only recently becoming part of an established body of knowledge. While the PSIs do not detail the specific negotiations that lead to charges brought in our white-collar crime cases, we are able to examine the end result of that process across the different crime categories.[12]

Decisions on these issues are, of course, based in part upon the facts of the offenses. A person committing a single theft of money from a bank teller's drawer cannot be charged with multiple counts, nor can he or she be charged with antitrust activities. Many of our offenses are not so clear cut, however. As we saw in chapter 2, sometimes two quite similar crimes are charged under different statutes. A single act, or series of acts, can violate a number of statutes. For example, 11 percent of those in our sample whose major charge is not bribery, commit crimes that in fact did involve bribery, and 8 percent of offenders whose main charge is not bank embezzlement are involved in embezzlements (though not necessarily from banks).

Prosecutors decide which statutes to use by considering two often contradictory needs, the need to get a charge that will stick and the need to get a charge to which the defendant will plead guilty. Among our white-collar crime categories, tax violators are most likely to be charged with only one offense, and securities violators are most likely to be charged with multiple offenses (see table 5.5). Indictment under

11. See Connie Bruck, *The Predator's Ball* (New York: Penguin Books, 1988).

12. Because of the tentative nature of our data, we are hesitant here to make any broad comparisons between white-collar and common crimes.

Table 5.5. Indications of Bargaining between the Defense and the Prosecution

	Percent Charged with One Offense	N[4]	Percent Charged with One Count	N[4]	Percent Charged by Information Only[1]	N[4]
Securities Fraud[2]	65.0%	223	46.3%	188	27.2%	224
Bribery	77.4%	84	53.0%	83	27.7%	83
Mail Fraud	72.0%	189	18.1%	177	16.2%	185
False Claims	77.7%	157	31.8%	154	20.8%	154
Credit Fraud	87.3%	157	37.1%	151	24.8%	153
Antitrust[2]	92.3%	117	87.6%	89	20.2%	114
Tax Fraud	93.8%	210	18.0%	200	28.9%	204
Bank Embezzlement	91.5%	201	49.2%	189	29.2%	195
All White-Collar Crimes[3]	83.4%	1,090	34.7%	1,038	24.5%	1,066
Common Crimes	83.8%	210	39.1%	197	18.1%	204

[1] In a small number of cases defendants were charged by a combination of informations and indictments.
[2] Includes the national sample of securities and antitrust offenders. See Appendix 1.
[3] Includes the basic sample only. See Appendix 1.
[4] N represents the number of individuals with nonmissing information for the variable. See Appendix 1.

a single statute may indicate a higher likelihood that negotiations have taken place than indictment under multiple statutes, though this part of the charging process is a complex one, and such an inference could be wrong for some cases.

As this reasoning would suggest, antitrust violators, who are most likely to retain private counsel and who are at the top of our offense hierarchy, are also among the most likely to be charged with only one offense. At the same time those next-most-likely to retain private counsel, the securities violators, are least likely to be charged with a single offense. So the number of offenses charged is not simply a function of the complexity of the crime or whether private counsel has been retained. As we would expect, the most common secondary offense to be charged is conspiracy, which is present in 15 percent of the charging instruments.

For each charged offense there is a list of specific occasions on which the offense is alleged to have taken place. Each occasion is called a count. The prosecution has discretion in the number of counts charged, and these, too, are subject to negotiation. In many cases a prosecutor may agree to reduce the number of counts in exchange for information or other concessions. The antitrust cases are the most likely to be charged with a single count, followed by bribery and bank embezzlement. The offenders charged with tax fraud and mail fraud are the least likely to face single-count indictments.[13]

Often prosecutors will charge a single count of a single offense in exchange for helpful information. This charge may place severe limits on the sentencing judge's ability to impose a harsh sentence. For example, in antitrust cases, a single conspiracy may exist over several years, involve numerous specific actions, and may even change in form over the years, yet these offenders are almost always charged with a single offense and a single count. Of those offenders who provide information about others to authorities, 42 percent are charged with one count of a single offense, compared to fewer than 30 percent of those who do not cooperate with the government.

13. The number of counts charged against tax offenders is interesting in light of the fact that they are generally charged with single offenses. This may reflect the nature of the tax law and of tax offenses. Each tax statute is clearly distinct from the others in the type of activity it restricts, and in most cases each instance of illegal behavior is quite distinct, since it is defined by an annual or quarterly filing of forms. There is much less ambiguity for the negotiators to manipulate than there is under the other statutes.

Table 5.6. The Use of Informations to Charge White-Collar
Criminals, by District

District	Percent Charged by Information Only	N
Southern New York[1]	38.9%	221
Maryland	21.3%	108
Northern Georgia	14.5%	131
Northern Texas	22.7%	154
Northern Illinois	16.1%	137
Central California[1]	17.7%	192
Western Washington	34.7%	121
Total	24.5%	1,064

[1] Figures include offenders in the basic sample only. See Appendix 1.

In the federal system, the defendant is charged by either an
"indictment" or an "information." An indictment is returned by a
grand jury based upon evidence presented to it by the prosecutor. An
information is issued by the prosecutor. Felonies—technically, those
offenses that may result in imprisonment for more than one year—
must be charged by an indictment, unless the defendant consents to
being charged by an information. The use of an information is thus,
in our sample of convicted felons, an indication that at least minimal
communication between the prosecutor and the defendant has occurred.

In fact, almost one in four of our white-collar criminals are
charged through an information. Well over half of the informations
include only one count. This contrasts with indictments, where only
about 20 percent contain single counts. The use of informations as
opposed to indictments does not vary greatly among our offenses,
with the exception of their relatively infrequent use for mail-fraud
offenders.

The use of informations varied among judicial districts (see table
5.6). In our sample, more than one-third of those convicted in the
Southern District of New York and the Western District of Washington are charged by informations, while fewer than 20 percent
of the defendants from Central California, Northern Illinois, and

Northern Georgia are charged in this way. This variation may suggest a differing degree of receptivity to the use of informations by different prosecutors' offices or differences in other practices between districts. For example, in the Southern District of New York the high rate of use of informations was in part due to the fact that at the time of our study a charge by information enabled the defendant to select the judge who would hear the case.

Facing the Judge

Once charges are filed, a defendant faces a judge for the first time. At this point, one of the critical strategic moves in criminal defense work—the selection of the "right" judge—comes into play. Experienced prosecutors and defense attorneys are aware of the reputations of some judges for leniency and of others for harshness. Clearly, defense attorneys want their cases heard by judges who are believed to be more lenient.

Although the system is designed to make such "judge shopping" in the federal system difficult, at the time our sample was drawn defense counsel could exert some control over the assignment to a judge by careful timing of the filing of a plea.[14] If one common perception is correct, private attorneys should have more resources—most notably paid time—to devote to this process, as they do to the other pretrial negotiations, and thus greater success at "judge shopping" than attorneys from the public defender's office.

For forty-two of the eighty-six judges represented in our sample we have enough information on their sentencing patterns to classify them, in comparison with other judges, as either harsh, average, or lenient in the treatment of white-collar-crime offenders.[15] Thus, we can examine the relationship between the type of attorney the defen-

14. In recent years strict random allocation of judges has been attempted in a number of districts. See Arnold H. Lubasch, "'Shopping' for Judges Is Curbed," *New York Times,* May 1, 1987, sec. B, 1; and "Judge Shopping in Federal Court: Lawyers Quest for Leniency," *New York Times,* March 4, 1988, sec. B, 1.

15. All judges were within the seven districts. For twenty-two defendants, the judge was not identified. Only judges with ten or more cases without missing values for the variables in the probability of imprisonment model presented in chapter 6 were rated.

Table 5.7. Type of Judge for White-Collar Offenders, by Type of Counsel[1]

	Lenient	Average	Harsh	N[2]
Private Attorney	5.1%	85.6%	9.3%	257
Court-Appointed	8.5%	84.5%	7.0%	71
Public Defender or Legal Aid	15.3%	67.8%	16.9%	198

[1]Includes basic sample plus additional securities within the seven districts. See Appendix 1.

[2]N represents the number of individuals with nonmissing information for these variables.

dant has and whether he or she is sentenced by a harsh, average, or lenient judge.[16]

Our findings, while providing support for the existence of judge shopping, suggest that there is not a simple relationship between legal resources and judge choice. Private attorneys, both retained and court appointed, are indeed more successful in avoiding harsh judges than are public defenders (see table 5.7). But they are less likely to have their clients come before the most lenient judges. Overall, the advantage of employing private counsel seems to lie not in the counsel's ability to get before light sentencers but in their efforts to keep clients from coming before the tough ones.[17]

Bail and Pretrial Custody

The first major decision the judge usually makes is whether the defendant should be allowed to remain free during the course of the legal proceedings. There were, at the time of our study, two primary

16. For each judge the mean predicted probability of imposing an imprisonment sanction using the prediction model in chapter 6 was calculated. The difference between this score and the actual proportion of defendants sentenced to incarceration defined the judge's score on the leniency scale. Lenient judges were more than one standard deviation above the overall mean for judges, while harsh judges were more than one standard deviation below the mean.

17. Elin Waring, David Weisburd, Stanton Wheeler, and Eben Werber, "The Impact of Judicial Variation on White Collar Crime Sentencing." Paper presented to the Law and Society Association, June 1987.

legal reasons why a judge could detain a defendant: either he or she presented a risk of nonappearance for later proceedings or was deemed likely to attempt to obstruct justice (for example, by destroying evidence).

A defendant who is viewed as likely to flee may be required to post an appearance bond. If unable to post the bond, the defendant may be held in custody prior to trial. Generally, judges appear to think that our white-collar criminals present much less risk of nonappearance than our common criminals (table 5.8). The generally more stable employment situations of white-collar defendants, along with the presence of other characteristics associated with responsibility and respectability, explain why one-quarter of these offenders are released on personal recognizance.

Many of the remaining white-collar-crime criminals in our sample have the resources required to post bond. Only one in eight offenders charged with white-collar crimes spends any time in custody prior to serving the sentence for their crime. This is true for fewer than one in twenty-five of the antitrust sample. In sharp contrast, one-third of those charged with one of our comparison common crimes serve time behind bars prior to serving their sentences.

For those offenders facing white-collar-crime charges who did serve time in custody, the length of the detention is minimal compared to the time served by those charged with common crimes. If required to spend time in custody, three-quarters of the white-collar criminals spend a week or less in jail. Fewer than half of the common criminals in pretrial custody are so fortunate. Seldom—just 17 percent of the time—does a white-collar offender serve more than a month in pretrial custody, but almost half of the common criminals do so. Pretrial treatment is thus one instance in which white-collar offenders are treated less harshly than other criminals.[18]

Choosing between Plea and Trial

A commonly accepted, though widely criticized, part of the American justice system is the process of plea bargaining. A defendant's

18. Many of these differences are explained by factors that might contribute to appearances of stability, such as defender assets and occupational and social stability. When controlling for such characteristics, we find that conviction for a common crime as opposed to a white-collar crime does not itself lead to a lower likelihood of bail being set.

Table 5.8. Pretrial Decisions by the Judge

	Percent Denied Bail	N^3	Percent Spending Any Time in Custody	N^3
Antitrust[1]	0.0%	111	3.6%	111
Securities Fraud[1]	1.4%	209	5.8%	208
Bribery	0.0%	80	9.0%	78
Bank Embezzlement	1.1%	189	10.1%	189
Tax Fraud	2.6%	190	13.7%	204
Credit Fraud	4.2%	144	17.4%	144
False Claims	2.8%	141	18.0%	150
Mail Fraud	6.1%	179	19.1%	168
All White-Collar Crimes[2]	1.7%	1,013	12.6%	1,090
Common Crimes	19.9%	201	34.2%	190

[1]Includes the national sample of securities and antitrust offenders. See Appendix 1.

[2]Includes the basic sample only. See Appendix 1.

[3]N represents the number of individuals with nonmissing information for the variable. See Appendix 1.

plea of guilty saves the government the expense of a trial and the risk of an acquittal. In return, the defendant gets some advantage, usually at time of sentencing. It is fair to say that plea bargaining, whatever its merits, is essential to the functioning of the criminal justice system. Indeed, in most jurisdictions, at least 90 percent of convicted defendants plead guilty.[19]

We might expect that figure to be somewhat lower in white-collar-crime cases, both because of their general complexity and because they often present very difficult problems of evidence and proof. The actual process of negotiation and decision making, like that of charge bargaining, is an intricate affair known best only by insiders. We can glean some information by examining the visible traces of the process, namely the formal plea of the defendant. Nearly a fifth of our white-collar criminals plead not guilty and go to trial (see table 5.9).

19. See *Sourcebook of Criminal Justice Statistics* (Washington, D.C.: GPO, 1988), 442.

Table 5.9. Not-Guilty Pleas

	Percent Who Pleaded Not Guilty	N[3]
Bank Embezzlement	7.0%	199
Antitrust[1]	12.8%	117
Credit Fraud	13.6%	154
False Claims	20.4%	157
Tax Fraud	21.1%	209
Mail Fraud	23.2%	190
Bribery	25.0%	84
Securities Fraud[1]	28.3%	223
All White-Collar Crimes[2]	18.3%	1,082
Common Crimes	4.8%	209

[1] Includes the national sample of securities and antitrust offenders. See Appendix 1.

[2] Includes the basic sample only. See Appendix 1.

[3] N represents the number of individuals with nonmissing information for the variable. See Appendix 1.

This far exceeds the rates found in most studies and is four times the rate of those in our common-crime sample.

There is great variation in the rate of going to trial among different types of white-collar defendants. Bank embezzlers resemble common criminals in that they rarely go to trial, and not-guilty pleas are even rarer in those cases that involve thefts by tellers. As noted earlier, they are often simple cases with clear evidence, and prosecutors may actively seek guilty pleas. The bank-embezzlers who do go to trial tend to be higher level officials involved in more complex crimes, for whom more is at stake—both in terms of possible sanctions and loss of social status—and in which the evidence is less straightforward.

At the other end of the distribution are the bribery and SEC offenders, of whom more than a quarter go to trial. The reasons for this are most likely twofold. On the one hand, the government may feel that its case is strong enough so that it does not need to make concessions. On the other, the defense may believe that it will be fully vindicated at trial and that it has nothing to gain by making any deals with the prosecution. In the bribery cases, for example, clear evidence is often gathered, but it comes many times from one of the parties to the bribe, often a witness of questionable character whose testimony may not be believed by a jury.

Generally, defendants facing relatively mild sanctions are less apt to proceed to trial. While this is one reason that our antitrust violators seldom go to trial, another lies in special aspects of the antitrust laws themselves. These laws specifically provide for punitive damages to be awarded civilly in the amount of three times the actual damages suffered as a result of the illegal conduct.[20] Because of this, antitrust offenders often make the special plea of nolo contendere.

By making this plea, defendants state not that they are guilty, but literally that the charges will not be contested. The effect on the criminal case is the same as if the defendant had pleaded guilty, but this plea cannot be used as prima facie evidence of liability in related civil litigation. Thus, by pleading nolo contendere, the defendant makes it much more difficult for victims to obtain civil damages.

The Personal Toll of the Process

The final step in the judicial process for defendants is the imposition of a sentence. This will be examined in depth in chapter 6. Before turning to that, however, we examine the personal impact that being accused of a white-collar crime has on our offenders up to the time of sentencing. The presumption of such a toll is sometimes the basis for arguments for leniency in the sentencing of white-collar criminals.

Many observers of the criminal-justice system believe that movement through the legal process takes a greater toll on white-collar offenders than on other criminals. Indeed, a number of scholars suggest that the effects of prosecution and conviction on the lives of white-collar defendants provide a greater punishment than the actual legal penalties they face.[21] Research on judicial attitudes shows

20. Offenders in our other crime categories may also be subject to civil damages, but these statutes generally do not specify such large dollar amounts.
21. See, for example, Michael Benson, "Collateral Consequences of Conviction for a White Collar Crime," Ph.D. diss., University of Illinois, 1982; and Wheeler, Mann, and Sarat, *Sitting in Judgment.*

that judges echo this concern about the suffering experienced by white-collar criminals in the legal system. For example, one federal judge interviewed in Wheeler, Mann, and Sarat's study *Sitting in Judgment* explains:

> First, the white-collar criminal by virtue of his conviction has suffered a loss of position, usually loss of employment, sometimes status in his profession, other times the ability to ever find employment in anything requiring a fidelity bond or what have you. Whereas the common street criminal hasn't had a career loss of a similar nature; indeed in some areas the conviction of a crime is some sort of a badge of maturity. Whereas, in a white-collar neighborhood, conviction for crime is generally going to cause economic hardship and a lot of social loss of prestige, and I think that is something you have to give weight to. If you take a man who has been a pillar of his community and has a good family, and no criminal background he's convicted of embezzling from a bank, he loses his job, he loses his home, and he probably loses his family, it often occurs and he also loses his future prospect of employment-he has already been punished fairly substantially. The ordinary street criminal hasn't suffered that kind of loss, there isn't that sort of thing that could be put on the scales. That is one distinction in white-collar sentencing.[22]

Another judge focused more specifically on how the return of an indictment and its attendant publicity would lead to special suffering in the case of white-collar defendants:

> There is no doubt about the fact that in most white-collar crimes as such the return of the indictment is much more traumatic than even the sentence. Pronouncing of the sentence is not as injurious to the person, his relationship to the community, to his family, as the return of the indictment. The return of the indictment in many instances causes a tremendous loss, is felt, the loss of business relationships, often the loss of jobs, of bank credit, a loss of friends, social status, occasionally loss of a wife, members of the family, children around the father, more when they hear that an indictment has been returned and he has been charged than they

22. Wheeler, Mann, and Sarat, *Sitting in Judgment,* 145–46.

do after they have gotten used to the idea and he is sentenced for it. There is no question about the fact that that is much more severe on the white-collar criminal than it is on the blue-collar defendant.[23]

Judges interviewed by Wheeler and his colleagues may be right in their belief that the legal process has negative effects on white-collar offenders. But there has been little empirical examination of this "fact," or the presumption that common-crime defendants and their families do not suffer, or suffer much less.[24] It could be argued that the empathy judges feel for defendants often similar to them in background may lead them to project their own feelings, the hurt or sense of humiliation they believe they would feel if it were happening to them, onto the defendants. Or, even if generally true, the effect might be differentially distributed among different types of white-collar offenders.

Given what judges say about the experiences of white-collar defendants in the legal process, it is not surprising to find that defense counsel, both orally and in sentencing memoranda, frequently argue that their clients have already suffered and that only minimal further punishments should be imposed. Virtually every sentencing memorandum we have seen includes some reference to suffering as a result of some form of secondary (that is, nonjudicial) sanctions. Here is one example from a memorandum prepared by attorneys in a case of tax fraud:

> Although he has never before been convicted of any offense, this single conviction, which has already been widely reported in the press, will irretrievably tarnish Mr. ———'s reputation in the community for honesty and integrity, which he has enjoyed until the present. Mr. ——— and his family have already suffered greatly from the shame, humiliation and agonized uncertainty which have attended this criminal investigation and prosecution. Mr. ——— has already paid ——— to the IRS in payment of taxes,

23. Ibid., 145.
24. Malcolm Feeley (*The Process Is the Punishment* [New York: Russell Sage, 1979]) suggests that middle-class defendants are more likely to fear the stigma of prosecution and conviction. See also Levi, *Regulating Fraud*, 322–30.

interest and penalties to be assessed and stands ready to make substantial additional payments. . . . The publicity resulting from Mr. ———'s plea of guilty, and knowledge of his guilty plea throughout the community have already benefited society by deterring others who may be tempted to commit similar violations of the law.

It is far easier to show the systematic presentation of the special and negative effects of the legal process on white-collar offenders, or of the belief in such an effect, than it is to develop documented evidence of it. On the one hand, *claims* of damage from the process may be calculated to win sympathy and may have little basis in reality. On the other hand, the PSI does not routinely record whether a defendant is harmed or not. It is only noted if brought formally to the attention of the probation officer, and thus the PSI might miss some unreported suffering. For this reason our findings on the personal toll of the process must be regarded as suggestive.

Even where evidence of some kind of physical or mental problem is clear, it may be difficult to sort out what portion should be attributed to the offense and what portion might have been a concomitant or even preexisting occurrence. One of the very few antitrust cases to go to trial gives evidence of some of these complexities. The offender was a thirty-five-year-old president of a real estate firm who, along with others at a meeting of a county board of realtors, agreed among themselves to raise their commission rates one percentage point. "Starting at the bottom in a small, one office firm in 1966, defendant had risen to sole owner within seven years." The defendant, a college graduate, had suffered a heart attack prior to the offense, and in the words of his physician, "had intermittent angina pectoris precipitated at times by more than ordinary exertion, but more often by emotional stress." He experienced an angina attack on the next-to-the-last day of trial. Since the offense he had been under the care of a psychiatrist. The psychiatrist diagnosed the defendant as a "cyclothymic personality, characteristically hypomanic," as revealed by recurring and alternating periods of depression and elation. The difficulties in sorting out the timing and reality of these problems, both for the probation officer and the researcher, are clear.

With these reservations and qualifications in mind, we searched the PSIS for any evidence indicating that an offender had experienced

Table 5.10. Any Reports of Suffering or Hardship as a Result of the
Offense

	Any Suffering Reported[4]	N[3]
Antitrust[1]	23.9%	117
Bribery	58.3%	84
Securities Fraud[1]	70.2%	225
Tax Fraud	60.0%	210
False Claims	52.9%	157
Credit Fraud	65.0%	157
Mail Fraud	57.7%	189
Bank Embezzlement	87.1%	201
All White-Collar Crimes[2]	64.4%	1,090
Common Crimes	25.2%	210

[1]Includes the national samples of securities and antitrust offenders. See Appendix 1.

[2]Includes the basic sample only. See Appendix 1.

[3]N represents the number of individuals with nonmissing information for this variable. See Appendix 1.

[4]Includes marriage or separation, physical or mental health deterioration, reports from various sources that the family has suffered, probation officer reports of suffering by the defendant, filings for personal or business bankruptcy, or being fired from job as a result of the discovery of the crime.

what is often termed secondary (or nonlegal) sanctions as a result of his or her prosecution and conviction. In particular, we looked for descriptions of suffering as related to employment, family relationships, or physical or mental health. We also recorded personal bankruptcies and the loss or bankruptcy of businesses.[25]

About two-thirds of our white-collar criminals are identified as experiencing some type of secondary sanction between the time that legal proceedings began and sentencing (see table 5.10). Though on average they are much more likely to show such evidence than our

25. Of course, these events often are of benefit to the offender since they provide protection from creditors or may raise the cash necessary to mount a legal defense. Nevertheless, we assumed that such financial events could cause difficulties or embarrassment later on.

comparison group of common-crime offenders, as we will see below, the differences between the white-collar and common-crimes we examine are not always great. Moreover, on some dimensions, there is often very little suffering noted by any of the offenders in our sample.

It is interesting that the antitrust offenders (who are closest to the ideal picture of white-collar criminals) suffer secondary sanctions least often, while those who in many respects least resemble it (bank embezzlers) suffer them the most often. The securities violators report suffering more frequently than persons in any of the remaining categories.

The most objective evidence we have concerns the offender's employment during the offense and the legal proceedings; we collected information about the employer's immediate reaction to discovering that the defendant was involved in the offense and the jobs the defendant held during the offense and during the legal proceedings. The experiences of our offenders vary a great deal between offense categories. Bank embezzlers suffer the most in terms of employment (table 5.11). Most are terminated. Fully a third of those who had been employed during the offense are unemployed during the course of the legal proceedings, and some 77 percent hold jobs of lower status during the legal proceedings than they did during the crime. While none of the other offense categories evidence employment problems to this degree, a substantial proportion of offenders in each category, with the exception of antitrust and tax, are fired, leave their jobs, or become unemployed during legal proceedings.

Few of those in the white-collar-crime sample file for personal bankruptcy. While the overall percentage who do so is much larger than that found in the common-crime group, it should be remembered that comparatively few common criminals are employed during the time they commit their crimes.

An often cited secondary sanction for white-collar-crime defendants is the loss of their businesses. Indeed some of those in our white-collar-crime sample who own businesses are reported to have experienced a business bankruptcy during legal proceedings. Credit-fraud offenders and securities violators are most likely to lose their businesses, and antitrust violators and bribery offenders are least likely. Those convicted of mail and tax fraud, and false claims and bank embezzlement form an intermediate category.

Evidence of family suffering is found in statements made by the

Table 5.11. Employment and Financial Changes between the Time of the Offense and the Legal Proceedings

	Percent Immediately Fired or Leaving Job upon Discovery of Crime	Percent Who Became Unemployed[1]	Percent Who Lowered Duncan Score	N[2]	Percent Going into Personal Bankruptcy	N[3]	Percent of Owners or Sole Proprietors Who Lost or Had Bankrupt Businesses	N[4]
Antitrust[5]	4.5%	1.8%	12.5%	112	0.0%	117	8.3%	48
Bribery	16.2%	9.5%	21.6%	74	0.0%	84	10.5%	38
Securities Fraud[5]	14.4%	13.9%	42.3%	208	4.9%	225	57.9%	114
Tax Fraud	8.4%	12.1%	22.6%	190	3.8%	210	26.5%	102
False Claims	24.2%	21.8%	36.9%	124	3.2%	157	19.5%	41
Credit Fraud	31.4%	22.9%	44.9%	118	4.5%	158	59.6%	52
Mail Fraud	23.2%	27.5%	45.7%	138	2.6%	190	46.8%	62
Bank Embezzlement	76.8%	35.1%	76.8%	194	1.5%	201	33.3%	12
All White-Collar Crimes[6]	24.7%	19.0%	40.7%	1,090	2.8%	1,090	14.5%	359
Common Crimes	26.1%	34.8%	63.8%	69	0.0%	210	0.0%	2

[1]Some who lost their jobs upon discovery or later were at new jobs by the time of the legal proceedings. Does not include those who were unemployed at both times.
[2]Includes all employed individuals with known occupational titles during the time of the actual offense.
[3]Includes all members of the sample used.
[4]Includes all owners and sole proprietors of businesses.
[5]Includes the national sample of securities and antitrust offenders. See Appendix 1.
[6]Includes the basic sample only. See Appendix 1.

defendant, by the probation officer, or sometimes by members of the defendant's family. Of course, just as the assertion that such suffering has taken place does not necessarily mean that it has, the fact that no mention is made does not mean that the defendant's family life has not suffered. Mention of some negative effect on family life is found in almost one-fifth of the PSIs in white-collar-crime cases, and in about one-third as many of the common-crime investigations (table 5.12).

We can see how serious the possible impact of criminal-justice processing is by examining divorce and separation rates from the onset of the offense through convictions and preparation of the PSI. Less than 1 percent of the antitrust offenders go through separation or divorce, and they are also among the least likely to report family suffering. In contrast, credit-fraud offenders, though seldom reporting family suffering, have a marital break-up rate of more than 20 percent, the highest in our sample. This may illustrate the potentially misleading character of self-reports of suffering.

The PSIs were also searched for evidence of deterioration in either physical or mental health. Again, these were not questions for which answers were routinely recorded. Overall, some 18 percent of the white-collar-crime PSIs contain statements referring to a negative change in health, and these were fairly evenly split between physical and mental deterioration, with fewer than 2 percent mentioning both (table 5.13). This strikes us as surprisingly small, given the frequent mention of both physical and mental deterioration in some of the most highly publicized white-collar-crime cases, again indicating the problems with relying on such cases as the basis of generalization. In this regard, it is interesting that common criminals, while on average less likely than those in the white-collar crime categories to be linked to these forms of suffering, are reported to experience them more often than antitrust violators.

The probation officer can report his or her own evaluation of suffering by the offender, and this is our final indicator of the possible impact of the legal process. As table 5.14 shows, such comments are present in relatively few PSIs, though again probation officers are much more likely to note this about white-collar criminals than about common-crime offenders (table 5.14).

Within the white-collar crime categories the sharply different placement of securities and antitrust violators is most notable. The former lie near the top in most indicators of secondary sanctions,

Table 5.12. Reports of Suffering by the Offender's Family

	Reported by					Separated or Divorced[4]	Base N[1]
	Probation Officer	Offender	Offender's Family	At Least One Source	Base N[1]		
Antitrust[2]	2.6%	6.8%	5.1%	12.0%	117	0.9%	109
Bribery	7.1%	10.7%	7.1%	20.2%	84	10.2%	59
Securities Fraud[2]	9.3%	13.3%	16.9%	31.1%	225	15.9%	176
Tax Fraud	5.2%	9.5%	7.2%	21.4%	210	16.2%	154
False Claims	2.6%	8.3%	7.0%	15.9%	157	18.2%	88
Credit Fraud	3.8%	5.7%	6.3%	18.4%	158	21.2%	85
Mail Fraud	2.1%	5.3%	6.8%	14.7%	190	9.3%	97
Embezzlement	7.0%	9.0%	6.0%	16.4%	201	8.8%	102
All White-Collar Crimes[3]	6.1%	9.8%	6.5%	18.5%	1,090	15.3%	662
Common Crimes	3.3%	2.4%	2.4%	6.2%	210	11.3%	53

[1] N represents the number of individuals with nonmissing information for this variable. See Appendix 1.
[2] Includes the national samples of securities and antitrust offenders. See Appendix 1.
[3] Includes the basic sample only. See Appendix 1.
[4] Includes only those who were married at the start of the offense who were separated or divorced between the time of the offense and the time of sentencing.

Table 5.13. Reported Deterioration of Health between the Time of
the Crime and Sentencing

	Physical Health	Mental Health	Combination of Physical and Mental Health	N^1
Antitrust[2]	6.2%	3.9%	1.9%	117
Bribery	9.8%	13.2%	0.0%	84
Securities Fraud[2]	11.5%	10.0%	3.6%	225
Tax Fraud	11.5%	7.9%	3.7%	210
False Claims	7.7%	2.8%	1.4%	157
Credit Fraud	7.3%	10.4%	0.7%	158
Mail Fraud	11.1%	7.6%	0.6%	190
Bank Embezzlement	2.0%	11.7%	0.5%	201
All White-Collar Crimes[3]	8.1%	9.7%	1.3%	1,090
Common Crimes	5.8%	6.6%	2.6%	210

[1]N represents the number of individuals with nonmissing information for
this variable. See Appendix 1.

[2]Includes the national samples of securities and antitrust offenders. See
Appendix 1.

[3]Includes the basic sample only. See Appendix 1.

while the latter are consistently least likely to indicate suffering
through the legal process. In some sense these findings both support
and contradict the view that the white-collar defendants at the top of
the hierarchy of white-collar crime will suffer most. Differences in the
quality and strategies of legal representation for the two groups of
offenders may explain some of these differences. The well-established
respectability of the antitrust offenders also may protect them and
their families, while the shallowness of the respectability of the securities violators becomes apparent under the spotlight of a criminal
investigation.

Perhaps it is the case that antitrust violators, who steal *for* their
companies and actually provide the services they say they do, fail to
receive the stigma that attaches to those who steal *from* their companies. The antitrust violators remain owners or officers in their
companies, with little change in their professional status, in great
part because while acting against the community they have acted for
their businesses. In contrast, securities offenders and bank embez-

Table 5.14. Probation Officer Reports of Suffering by the Offender
as a Result of the Legal Process

	Suffering Reported	N[1]
Antitrust[2]	2.6%	117
Bribery	15.5%	84
Securities Fraud[2]	8.4%	225
Tax Fraud	8.6%	210
False Claims	8.9%	157
Credit Fraud	5.7%	158
Mail Fraud	5.3%	190
Bank Embezzlement	10.5%	201
All White-Collar Crimes[3]	8.7%	1,090
Common Crimes	1.9%	210

[1]N represents the number of individuals with nonmissing information for this variable. See Appendix 1.
[2]Includes the national samples of securities and antitrust offenders. See Appendix 1.
[3]Includes the basic sample only. See Appendix 1.

zlers are likely to suffer more, the former because their crimes are often against their own clients, the latter because they steal from their employers.

These materials on the toll exacted by the legal process provide a beginning from which other empirical inquiries can build. Our assessment is that they do not supply sufficient evidence to either support or reject the hypothesis that involvement with the legal process is in itself a major form of punishment for white-collar criminals.[26] Though they are more likely to suffer than our comparison group of common criminals, in all but the financial categories (where common-crime defendants have little to lose anyway) the differences we find are not large in absolute terms.

For three reasons our findings must be viewed as exploratory at

26. Of course, we do not here deal with the question of whether any defendant's sentence, whether white collar or not, *should* take into account the amount of suffering during the process. Certainly, many federal judges believe that such process effects as loss of professional license and professional reputation should be reflected in the sentence. See Wheeler, Mann, and Sarat, *Sitting in Judgment,* 144–51.

best. First, the PSIS record only what people happened to say. They were not designed to assess the human toll in each individual case. The fact that the record does not reveal suffering does not mean it did not occur. Second, accounts by defendants or family members can be self-serving, especially if they believe that reported suffering may lighten their sentence.

Third, we do not have a good sense for the causal direction of these relationships. Although our records reflect changes during the process, we do not know whether they were already underway before the start of the crime. Perhaps a shaky business and an unhappy marriage precipitate involvement in a crime, or conversely, the revelation of involvement in a crime may be the last straw that breaks up a shaky marriage or bankrupts a marginal business. However, there is good reason, based on anecdotal accounts, to believe that some offenders have experienced great hardship and suffering as they move from investigation through indictment and conviction and that by the time of sentencing the process really has provided a kind of punishment. But to know for which offenders this operates, and how deeply, we must await longitudinal studies designed specifically to assess such impacts.

Our examination of the movement of white-collar criminals through the legal process has been tentative in great part because the PSIS are not an ideal data source for this purpose.[27] Our results

27. Having attempted to mine the presentence investigation reports for evidence about these processes, we are struck with the need for more routine and systematic data collection. In the course of preparing their presentence investigation reports, probation officers pick up a lot of information, but often it seems to be hit or miss. We do not propose converting probation officers into social scientists, but the addition of a handful of standardized questions on some of these topics would provide us with a much stronger base than is currently available for learning about the stages that intervene between the onset of the crime and the ultimate sentence of the criminal. As the officials charged with preparing the presentence investigation report, the probation officers are in a position to record information systematically. Although attached to the courts, in theory they have neither the vested interest and bias of prosecutor or defense counsel, nor the Solomonic task of judge. They are thus in a unique position to contribute to our knowledge about the criminal-justice process, although they may bring their individual prejudices, as well as shared professional ideologies, to the recording of the information. For a

suggest that the contradictory images of great suffering and privileged advantage associated with white-collar crime defendants overstate their real experiences in the legal system. Access to private attorneys and stable community reputations and positions do provide advantages to white-collar defendants. But their social and economic positions appear to lead them to experience more of certain secondary sanctions than other criminals. However, neither the advantages nor the suffering are as great as one might expect given the rhetoric that has surrounded white-collar-crime prosecution.

discussion of some of the problems inherent in presentence investigation reports, see Todd Clear, Val B. Clear, and William D. Burrell, *Offender Assessment and Evaluation: The Presentence Investigation Report* (Cincinnati: Anderson, 1989).

6

Sentencing

We now come to the final stage of our analysis, the sentencing of convicted defendants by federal judges. Unlike our discussion in earlier chapters, where the absence of strong theoretical models led us to develop our understanding of white-collar crimes and criminals with reference primarily to our own data, the arena of sentencing behavior allows us to test models of the sentencing process that have been strongly advocated by others. Indeed, as a topic of research and theoretical discussion, sentencing has long been a subject of heated debate, with lawyers and scholars offering a series of carefully reasoned though often antagonistic images of how judicial sentencing works.

Lawyers and social scientists have each led attacks on sentencing practices, although their definition of the problems and their critiques of the system are very different. The lawyers' attack was strongly stated in the early 1970s by federal judge Marvin Frankel in his influential book *Criminal Sentences: Law without Order*.[1] Judge Frankel challenged the enormous discretion granted to sentencing judges and the absence of any acceptable standards or guidelines for the use of that discretion. His critique centered on the degree to

1. New York: Hill and Wang, 1972.

which judges and courts differ in the criteria used in sanctioning. Sociologists, in contrast, have focused less on arbitrariness and the absence of standards, and more on the possibilities of systematic bias and discrimination.[2] Particular concern has revolved around the possibility of social-class bias in sentencing as part of a more general proposition predicting heavier imposition of any legal controls on those further down the social hierarchy.

Our study was informed by these earlier critiques of judicial sentencing behavior. But we also set out to examine the sanctioning experience as it is described by those who make sentencing decisions. In a companion study, Stanton Wheeler, Kenneth Mann, and Austin Sarat conducted detailed qualitative interviews of federal judges, most of whom were located in three of the districts in our sample.[3] Their queries about the sentencing of white-collar offenders yielded an image of the way judges arrive at sentences different than those of earlier studies. Unlike scholars who saw mostly discrimination or an absence of standards, they found a considerable degree of consensus concerning the broad principles that should influence sentencing behavior. Although they stress that this consensus on principles does not produce agreement on actual sentences, their model of judicial sanctioning identifies a common sociolegal culture grounded in concepts that have been part of Anglo-American criminal law and jurisprudence for centuries.

Imprisonment Sanctions

It has long been assumed that white-collar criminals receive a significant advantage at the time of sentencing.[4] In particular,

2. For example, see William J. Chambliss and Robert B. Seidman, *Law, Order and Power* (Reading, Mass.: Addison-Wesley, 1971); Alan J. Lizotte, "Extra-Legal Factors in Chicago's Criminal Courts: Testing the Conflict Model of Criminal Justice," *Social Problems* 25 (1978):564–80.

3. Stanton Wheeler, Kenneth Mann, and Austin Sarat, *Sitting in Judgment* (New Haven: Yale University Press, 1988). Their study included many judges in the Southern District of New York, the Northern District of Illinois, and the Central District of California.

4. This, of course, has been the case since Sutherland's day (see Sutherland, *White Collar Crime: The Uncut Version* [New Haven: Yale University Press, 1983]). For an interesting discussion of recent attitudes toward the sanctioning of corporate white-collar defendants, see Kip Schlegel, *Just Des-*

they are seen as less likely to be imprisoned than common-crime offenders, and more likely to receive short prison stays if they are imprisoned.[5] Indeed, there is a common perception among laypeople that few white-collar offenders go to jail at all. This view is wrong (see table 6.1). Even a fifth of the antitrust violators go to prison, though most for only short times. Securities offenders, who also lie at the top of our hierarchy of white-collar crime, go to prison two-thirds of the time, more than those in any other crime category in our study.

Almost half of our common criminals are sentenced to some jail time, a figure close to that for other nonviolent common criminals (though much lower than that for violent crimes, such as robbery or serious assaults)[6] and slightly higher (49.7 percent, versus 46.4 percent) than that for white-collar-crime offenders. There is great variation among the white-collar-crime categories. Antitrust offenders, for example, are less than half as likely as the common-crime offenders to go to prison, while those convicted of securities violations, or tax or mail fraud, are sentenced to prison more often than the comparison common criminals.[7]

When our common criminals are sentenced to prison they get longer sentences than the white-collar offenders.[8] Among white-collar offenders, antitrust violators again receive the most

---

serts for the Corporate Criminal (Boston: Northeastern University Press, 1990).

5. See, for example, William Chambliss, *Criminal Law in Action* (Santa Barbara, Calif.: Hamilton, 1975); Whitney North Seymour, "1973 Sentencing Study for the Southern District of New York," *New York State Bar Journal* 45:163–71.

6. *Sourcebook of Criminal Justice Statistics* (Washington, D.C.: GPO, 1988), 444.

7. Our findings are generally consistent with those reported by John Hagan and Ilene Nagel in their 1982 study of sentencing in the Southern District of New York. For example, they note: "Defendants convicted of such crimes as mail fraud, fraudulent claims against government agencies, and tax fraud were sentenced with a severity that was similar to common crimes, while many (if not most) other white-collar criminals, particularly those convicted of price-fixing, received more lenient treatment" ("White-Collar Crime, White-Collar Time: The Sentencing of White-Collar Offenders in the Southern District of New York," *American Criminal Law Review* 20 [1982]:279).

8. The only exception to this occurs when we examine the mean sentence given to imprisoned mail-fraud offenders. This anomaly occurs because of a few very long sentences.

Table 6.1. Imprisonment Sanctions Imposed

Offense	Percent Receiving Imprisonment Sanctions	Mean Prison Sentence (Months)	Standard Deviation	Median Prison Sentence (Months)	Longest Prison Sentence Imposed	N^2
Antitrust[1]	19.2%	1.8	0.4	2	2	26
Securities Fraud[1]	67.2%	19.6	25.1	12	144	64
Bribery	36.6%	24.7	46.2	6	180	82
False Claims	40.1%	18.8	22.3	6	84	157
Mail Fraud	55.1%	48.2	119.4	18	976	185
Credit Fraud	47.1%	13.5	12.9	6	60	153
Tax Fraud	58.9%	9.3	13.0	5	84	207
Bank Embezzlement	30.8%	13.0	16.5	6	60	195
All White-Collar Crimes[3]	46.4%	21.3	58.7	6	976	1,069
Common Crimes	49.7%	25.1	22.7	24	120	201

[1] Includes individuals in the basic sample. The national figures are comparable.
[2] N represents the number of individuals with nonmissing information for the variable.
[3] Includes the basic sample only. See Appendix 1.

lenient sentences. Imprisoned tax offenders, who are among those most likely to go to prison, receive relatively short prison stays.

The length of some of the white-collar-crime sentences is particularly interesting. One securities violator, for example, received a fifteen-year sentence. He was fifty-four years of age, steadily employed, had no prior record, a college degree, and "frequently attends [religious] services." A mail-fraud offender received the harshest sentence in our study—fifty years imprisonment (more than twice that imposed on any of the common criminals in our sample). This fifty-one-year-old man, who grew up in a "stable home environment receiving adequate physical and emotional support from his parents," owned two insurance companies, which were used to carry out his offense. He was an honorably discharged war veteran. Although only a high school graduate, he does not fit stereotypes of common criminality. Nonetheless, he had two prior federal convictions, and according to his presentence investigation he "has continually become involved in schemes to defraud others of their financial resources. He has failed to learn from previous mistakes and it appears a pattern of behavior has been established in Mr. ———'s life that will be difficult to break."

Clearly, a simple review of the sentences meted out to offenders cannot answer the complex questions we raised at the outset. Our discussion below will center on the variability in white-collar-crime sentencing itself. Though we will return later in the chapter to a comparison of white-collar and common-crime sentencing, our initial problem will be to analyze the extent to which judicial behavior in white-collar sentencing fits the three models we outlined earlier.

Modeling Sentencing Decisions

While consistency and regularity in sentencing behavior are at the core of our legal system's ideals, the model of chaos and disarray suggested by Judge Frankel and others predicts that people with identical characteristics and convicted of identical crimes will receive differing legal sanctions. In this model, judges respond to their own biases and moods, which will vary from judge to judge. The only consistency in sanctioning is the inconsistency of judicial behavior. Punishments will seem arbitrary and bear little relationship to the crime committed. In statistical terms this model means that we would expect little success in predicting the severity of judicial sanctions from knowledge of an offender's crime and background.

The discrimination model prevalent in sociological critiques of sanctioning suggests that judges are influenced all too strongly by the social backgrounds and positions of defendants who stand before them. Whereas the former perspective criticizes the inconsistency of sentencing practices, here the concern is with discrimination against those who are disadvantaged and powerless. In this perspective social class and social status play central roles in the reality of sentencing behavior. The expectation is that those of higher social standing and class position, irrespective of their prior conduct or present criminal behavior, will be treated more leniently than others. But beyond aspects of status and class, those who are perceived as of lower "rank" in society, for example racial and ethnic minorities, are believed to face harsher treatment throughout the criminal justice system.[9]

In contrast to models of chaos and disarray or of systematic discrimination, the process of sentencing described by Wheeler, Mann, and Sarat focuses on the degree to which judicial sanctions are determined by common sociolegal norms. They found that in making sentencing decisions judges draw upon a common body of legal principles. These principles are deeply rooted in Anglo-American law. One is the principle of seriousness: a more serious offense deserves a more severe sanction. A second is the principle of blameworthiness: the more blameworthy an individual, the more deserving he or she is of a harsher punishment.[10] A third is the principle of consequences: judges should consider the effects of the sentence both on others (that is, deterrence) and on the offender and his or her immediate circle.

The legal norms, however, do not operate in a vacuum. Seriousness and blameworthiness in particular are part of a broader set of normative judgments widely diffused throughout the society, and

9. See, for example, Donald Black, *The Behavior of Law* (New York: Academic Press, 1976), especially chapter 2; and Jeffrey H. Reiman, *The Rich Get Richer and the Poor Get Prison: Ideology, Class and Criminal Justice* (New York: John Wiley & Sons, 1979). See also Lizotte, "Extra-Legal Factors."

10. See Andrew Von Hirsch, *Doing Justice: The Choice of Punishment* (New York: Hill and Wang, 1976), 47, for a somewhat different approach to the concept of blameworthiness.

judges draw from this broad body, as well as from the legal principles themselves. Taken together, we call this the model of shared sociolegal norms.

This model provides an image of judicial sentencing that is different from the two other critiques. It deserves careful attention because it is a model that comes from those doing the sentencing. But for this very reason it might be seen as self-serving, for the judges are the focus of earlier criticisms and have most to gain by representing the sentencing process as predictable and equitable. Accordingly, we placed considerable emphasis on our efforts to model accurately the variables the judges themselves said were important in their sentencing decisions.

Some characteristics judges used to describe the harm resulting from an offense are fairly straightforward. First and most simply, there is the dollar loss attributed to a crime. Not surprisingly, the judges interviewed saw sharp distinctions between frauds involving only a few thousand dollars and those that net hundreds of thousands of dollars. Similarly, all things being equal, a crime that is localized within one particular neighborhood or community was not viewed as seriously as one that spread across state, regional, or national boundaries. Finally, judges argued that the more victims a crime affects, the more harm it causes the community.

Other characteristics judges used to evaluate the seriousness of a crime are more subtle. For example, the degree of complexity or sophistication shown in the commission of the offense—what we termed organizational complexity in chapter 4—is related to its seriousness. Offenses that involve several layers of organization or many offenders in a complicated relationship to one another, and that are organized to continue over a long period of time, are regarded as more serious than uncomplicated, one-shot crimes. The type of victim also counts. Theft of government property is one thing, whereas a fraudulent land deal that wipes out the savings of a retired couple is another.

As is the case with seriousness, judges argued that there are many ways of evaluating the blameworthiness of an individual who participates in a crime. The most obvious is the role a person plays in carrying out the illegality. Those who are leaders or instigators of a crime are more blameworthy than those only marginally involved.

There are other ways of assessing blameworthiness. Wheeler,

Mann, and Sarat suggest that judges commonly feel a fundamental ambivalence in the sentencing of white-collar defendants. On the one hand, such offenders are often individuals of high social status, and in the eyes of judges, they should thus feel a greater moral responsibility to the system that has benefited them. That is, the higher their social standing, the greater their blameworthiness. On the other hand, persons who occupy such positions often have impeccable records. They are not just free of taint but have made positive contributions to their communities. Just as their blameworthy status leads judges to argue that they are deserving of harsher sanctions, their praiseworthy past conduct is seen as a reason to reduce the severity of their sentences.

Judges also argue that there are several factors relating to the legal process that may legitimately influence the sentence imposed. Defendants who express remorse for their crimes or who cooperate with authorities should receive less harsh punishment. Some judges also feel that a defendant who spends the court's time and money by going to trial deserves a more severe sentence than one who pleads guilty.

There are two features of the judges' reports on sentencing that are difficult to model from the data in the PSIS. The first is their concern for deterrence. There are occasions when an important rationale for sentencing is to deter others, as well as to give effect to the seriousness and blameworthiness of a defendant's conduct. The PSIS seldom capture this judicial concern. Second, an aspect of blameworthiness that is only haphazardly reported is the nature of the defendant's underlying motive for the crime—for example, whether it was sheer greed or need born out of family problems.[11] With these two exceptions, we think we have caught the most important dimensions that federal judges draw upon in their sentencing decisions.

Why Some White-Collar Offenders Go to Prison and Others Do Not

We rely upon multivariate statistical analyses to explain why some of our offenders receive an imprisonment sanction while others

11. For an interesting attempt to extract such information from the PSIS see Mitchell Rothman and Robert Gandossy, "Sad Tales: The Accounts of White-Collar Defendants and the Decision to Sanction" (*Pacific Sociological Review* 25 [1982]:449–73).

Table 6.2. Description of the Variables Used in the Multivariate
Analysis of Sanctioning

Variable	Measurement
Drawn from the Discrimination Perspective	
Race	Binary, 1 = nonwhite, 0 = white
Sex	Binary, 1 = female, 0 = male
Age	Years of age
Socioeconomic Status	Interval scale ranging from 6.0 to 96.0. (Also relevant for the shared sociolegal norms perspective)
Net Worth	Assets minus liabilities. Used in the fine models only
Social Class	Five-category nominal variable describing the offender's social class. In the fine model it is a binary variable, 1 = unemployed, 0 = employed
Type of Counsel	Binary, 1 = public defender or court-appointed, 0 = private
Education	Six-level ordinal variable ranging from "grade school only" to "post-college education"
Respectability	Seven-level scale ranging from −3 to 3 (see chapter 4 for details). (Also relevant for the common sociolegal norms perspective)
Drawn from the Common Sociolegal Norms Perspective	
Organizational Complexity	Ten-level ordinal scale ranging from 4 to 13 (see chapter 4 for details)
Spread of Illegality	Four-level ordinal variable ranging from "local" to "national or international"
Number of Victims	Four-level ordinal scale ranging from "none" to "11 or more"
Type of Victim	Five-category nominal variable describing the type of victim
Dollar Victimization	Thirteen-level ordinal scale ranging from "0" to "over $2.5 million"
Maximum Exposure to Imprisonment	Maximum sentence permitted, in years
Maximum Exposure to Fine	Maximum fine permitted, in hundreds of dollars
Respectability	Seven-level scale ranging from −3 to 3 (see chapter 4 for details). (Also relevant for the discrimination perspective)

Table 6.2. *Continued*

Variable	Measurement
Prior Arrests	Total number of prior arrests
Most Serious Prior Conviction	Six-level ordinal scale ranging from "no prior convictions" to "highest felony offenses"
Role in Offense	Four-category nominal variable describing the offender's role in the crime
Source of Conviction	Binary, 1 = by trial, 0 = by a guilty plea
Socioeconomic Status	Interval scale ranging from 6.0 to 96.0. (Also relevant for the discrimination perspective)
Remorse	Binary, 1 = expressed remorse, 0 = no remorse expressed
Cooperation with Authorities	Binary, 1 = cooperated with authorities, 0 = did not cooperate
Drawn from the Chaos Perspective	
Judicial District	Seven-category nominal variable describing the district in which the offender was convicted
Statutory Offense	Eight-category nominal variable describing the offense of conviction

do not. Our choice of variables is informed by the three models of sentencing decision making described above (table 6.2). If the model of common sociolegal norms is correct, we should find the variables reflecting seriousness of crime and blameworthiness of offender to be predictive of sentencing decisions. If the discrimination model is correct, we should find variables reflecting the defendant's economic powerlessness and minority status to be good predictors. And if chaos reigns, we should have grave difficulty in predicting sentences at all.

Consistent with the model of sociolegal norms, the most important predictors of whether defendants go to jail or not relate to the seriousness of offense behavior. Both the magnitude of the take and its spread have statistically significant and strong effects upon the imprisonment decision (table 6.3).[12] All else being equal, there is a 20

12. Because we examine imprisonment—a binary dependent variable—a logit repression is used. See Mark Nerlove and S. James Press, *Univariate and Multivariate Loglinear and Logistic Models* (Santa Monica, Calif.: Rand Corp., 1973); Daniel McFadden, "Conditional Logit Analysis of Qualitative

Table 6.3. Logistic Regression Model of the Probability of
Imprisonment for Convicted White-Collar Offenders

Variable	Coefficient	Derivative at Mean
Intercept	−5.767***	−1.433
From the Discrimination Perspective		
Race	0.139	0.034
Sex	−1.271***	−0.316
Age	0.115*	0.029
Age squared	−0.001**	−0.000
Socioeconomic Status[2]	0.017***	0.005
Social Class[1]		
Owner	−0.285	−0.071
Officer	−0.873*	−0.217
Sole Proprietor	−0.058	−0.013
Manager	0.020	0.005
(Worker)		
Type of Counsel	−0.077	−0.019
Education	−0.097	−0.024
From the Common Sociolegal Norms Perspective		
Organizational Complexity	0.150**	0.037
Spread of Illegality	0.267*	0.066
Number of Victims	−0.154	−0.038
Type of Victim[1]		
Individual	−0.885*	−0.219
Government	−0.431	−0.107
Combination	−0.074	−0.018
Missing	−0.380	−0.094
(Business)		
Dollar Victimization	0.180***	0.045
Maximum Exposure to Prison	0.145***	0.036
Respectability	−0.176*	−0.044
Arrests	0.083**	0.021
Most Serious Prior Conviction	0.206*	0.051
Role in the Offense[1]	***	
Middle	−1.310**	−0.325
Minor	−1.036***	−0.257
Missing	−0.404	−0.100
(Major)		
Source of Conviction	0.309	0.077
Socioeconomic Status[2]	0.017***	0.004
Remorse	−0.301	−0.075
Cooperation with Authorities	−0.589	−0.146

Table 6.3. *Continued*

Variable	Coefficient	Derivative at Mean
From the Chaos Perspective		
District[1]	***	
Central California	0.338	0.084
Maryland	0.586	0.145
Southern New York	−0.119	−0.029
Northern Texas	1.118***	0.278
Northern Illinois	0.728*	0.181
Western Washington	0.334	0.083
(Northern Georgia)		
Offense[1]	***	
Bank Embezzlement	−0.320	−0.079
Tax Fraud	0.998**	0.247
Mail Fraud	−0.333	−0.082
Securities Fraud	0.838	0.208
False Claims	−0.489	−0.121
Bribery	−0.699	−0.174
Antitrust	−0.707	−0.176
(Credit Fraud)		

−2 Log-Likelihood = 999.81
Model Chi-Square = 328.91 with 42 Degrees of Freedom
(p < 0.001)
963 observations
*p < 0.05   **p < 0.01   ***p < 0.001

[1]For variables represented by a set of dummy variables, the excluded category is listed in parentheses. The overall significance of the variable is given opposite the name of the variable. The significance of differences between the individual dummy variables and the excluded category is given next to the dummy variable.

[2]Socioeconomic status is relevant for both the discrimination and the jurisprudential perspectives. It is used only once in calculating predicted values.

percent difference in the predicted likelihood of imprisonment for those who commit national versus localized crimes, and more than a 40 percent difference between those who net less than $500 from their crimes and those who gain more than $2.5 million (table 6.4).[13]

Choice and Behavior," in Paul Zarembka, ed., *Frontiers in Econometrics* (New York: Academic Press, 1974); and Eric A. Hanushek and John E. Jackson, *Statistical Methods for Social Scientists* (New York: Academic Press, 1977).

13. Although the logistic form is appropriate for the problem examined

Table 6.4. Selected Probability Estimates for Significant Variables in the In/Out Model

Independent Variables	Probability Estimates (%)[1]	Range[2]
Maximum Exposure to Prison		47
1 day–1 year	31	
1 year & 1 day–2 years	35	
4 years & 1 day–5 years	45	
14 years & 1 day–15 years	78	
Dollar Victimization		42
$101–500	27	
$2,501–5,000	38	
$10,000–25,000	47	
$25,001–100,000	51	
More than $2,500,000	69	
Organizational Complexity		29
4	31	
6	38	
8	45	
10	53	
12	60	
Spread of Illegality		20
Individual	40	
Local	47	
Regional	54	
National/International	60	
Duncan Socioeconomic Index		28
15.1	28	
49.4	42	
62	47	
66	49	
84	56	
Respectability		17
−2	59	
−1	55	
0	51	
1	46	
2	42	
Number of Arrests		18
0	41	
1	43	
2	45	
5	51	
9	59	

Table 6.4. *Continued*

Independent Variables	Probability Estimates (%)[1]	Range[2]
Most Serious Prior Conviction		21
None	41	
Minor Offense	46	
Low Felony	57	
Moderate Felony	62	
Role in Offense		24
Minor	27	
Missing	41	
Single/Primary	51	
Statutory Offense Category		40
Bribery	29	
Antitrust	29	
False Claims	34	
Mail Fraud	37	
Bank Embezzlement	38	
Credit Fraud	45	
SEC Fraud	66	
Tax Fraud	69	
Sex		38
Male	50	
Female	22	
Age		—[3]
22	39	
30	47	
40	50	
50	45	
61	33	
District		30
Southern New York	33	
Northern Georgia	35	
Central California	43	
Western Washington	43	
Maryland	50	
Northern Illinois	53	
Northern Texas	63	

[1] Estimates were calculated by holding all other variables at their means.
[2] Ranges were computed from fifth to ninety-fifth percentile scores.
[3] Because of the curvilinear effect the range is not measured.

The organizational complexity of an offense is also linked to offense severity. Those who commit more complex crimes are punished more severely than those who commit relatively simple crimes. A general indicator of seriousness, the maximum sentence allowed,[14] also has an important and statistically significant impact upon the likelihood of imprisonment, with those facing a potentially longer sanction much more likely to go to prison.

Two other variables that reflect seriousness in the minds of judges, the number of victims involved and the type of victim, do not have statistically significant effects on whether defendants go to prison. Our analysis suggests that once the spread of a crime's impact and its dollar victimization are accounted for judges do not give significant weight to other aspects of victimization.[15]

The blameworthiness of defendants (and their praiseworthiness) also has important impact upon the decision to imprison. Not surprisingly, given the importance of prior record in almost every study of sentencing decisions, the number of prior arrests and their serious-

---

here, the results are considerably more difficult to interpret than least-squares estimates. Unlike the linear model the logit estimates do not reflect a constant effect. Because of this, most of our discussion will center on probability estimates associated with levels of our measures when all of the other variables in the model are held at their mean. Thus, the logit response function of the probability of imprisonment P(imprisonment) = $1/(1+e^{-xb})$ is approximated by setting each independent variable except for the variable being estimated at its mean value.

14. The maximum sentence allowed for the crime reflects how seriously the crime has been defined by the legislature. It may also give an indication of the prosecutor's evaluation of the seriousness of the crime, as it is dependent on the number of counts charged and the choice of what charges to bring.

15. While type of victim is not significant overall, there is a significant difference between offenders with business victims and those with individual victims, with the latter less likely to go to jail than the former. It may be that, in terms of all crimes, judges consider crimes against persons more serious than crimes against property, but that, because of the peculiar nature of white-collar crimes in our sample, the distinction is not really relevant. Other factors may replace the persons/property distinction in white-collar sentencing. For example, some have proposed that an essential element in white-collar crime is the violation of trust (e.g., Susan Shapiro, "Collaring the Crime, Not the Criminal: 'Liberating' the Concept of White-Collar Crime," *American Sociological Review* 93 [1990]:623–58). It may be that such violations are more obvious in crimes against organizations than in crimes against individuals, although they certainly are present in both types of crimes.

ness is significantly related to the decision. An offender with no prior arrests but who is average in all other respects has about a 41 percent likelihood of being imprisoned. This may be contrasted with a similar defendant with nine arrests, at least one of them leading to serious felony conviction, who has a predicted likelihood of imprisonment of 78 percent.

An individual's social record also influences the probability of incarceration to a statistically significant degree. The more stable the individual appears, as measured by the respectability index, the less likely it is that he or she will go to prison. We also find that judges take into account the role that offenders play in carrying out a crime. Major figures are punished more harshly than others.

Perhaps the most surprising finding in our study, but one that was suggested by Wheeler, Mann, and Sarat, is that there is a strong positive relationship between social status and imprisonment.[16] Those higher up the status ladder are in fact more likely to be sent to prison than those of lower status. For example, our statistical model suggests that, all else being equal, doctors will have about a 30 percent greater likelihood of being imprisoned than truck drivers and almost a 13 percent greater likelihood than managers. Clearly, judges are taking seriously the idea that persons in positions of higher status and prestige are more deserving of imprisonment. The paradox of leniency and severity they allude to in their discussions of sentencing is in fact reflected in their actual sentencing behavior.

16. In the face of a result that is both strong and for some counterintuitive, we explored the distribution closely. It is quite "lumpy," with a high number of offenders (30 percent) in one SEI category—namely, real-estate agents and "manager" (otherwise undifferentiated). But the lump is just about in the middle of the distribution and does not materially weaken this finding. We then considered possible variables that might "explain away" the finding. The most obvious seemed to be that there could be a particular type of offense, or perhaps one or two particular districts, where something special is going on that would account for the results. Not so. We examined the data crime by crime and district by district (necessarily with fewer variables in the models) and found this to be a most stable result, one that runs in the same direction for every statutory type of offense and for every one of our seven districts save Western Washington, where the relationship is virtually zero. Other efforts to explain away the result proved equally fruitless. See also David Weisburd, Elin Waring, and Stanton Wheeler, "Class, Status, and the Punishment of White Collar Criminals," *Law and Social Inquiry* 50 2 (1990):223–43.

Although the judges interviewed by Wheeler and his colleagues mentioned several legal-process variables that can influence the sentence imposed, they were less consistent in describing this dimension of their model than others. This lack of consensus is generally reflected in our results. While cooperation with the authorities, expressions of remorse, and a guilty plea all reduce the probability of imprisonment in our sample, once the effects of other variables are removed, the results remain in the predicted direction but are neither strong nor statistically significant.

In contrast to the general consistency between the model of sentencing suggested by federal judges and our findings, there is little fit between the discrimination model and white-collar crime sentencing. Neither race, social class, nor type of counsel have statistically significant effects upon the sentencing decisions of judges.[17] Only if we were to view respectability as a class measure, rather than an indicator of social record, do we find support for the discrimination model. Indeed, for the other measures, the seemingly less powerful defendants are given an advantage. For example, we have already noted that those of higher status are more likely to be imprisoned. We also find that women are significantly less likely to be sentenced to prison than men,[18] and those who are young and old are less likely to be imprisoned than those of middle age.

17. One dimension of this problem, the victim/offender interaction, could not be modeled from the PSIS. For example, recent research on the use of capital punishment has found that the race of the victim is a significant predictor of whether a death penalty is imposed. See Samuel R. Gross and Robert Mauro, "Patterns of Death: An Analysis of Racial Disparities in Capital Sentencing and Homicide Victimization," *Stanford Law Review* 37(1):27–153; Raymond Paternoster, "Prosecutorial Discretion in Requesting the Death Penalty: A Case of Victim-Based Racial Discrimination," *Law and Society Review* 18 (3):437–78; Raymond Paternoster, "Race of Victim and Location of Crime: The Decision to Seek the Death Penalty in South Carolina," *Journal of Criminal Law and Criminology* 74 (3):754–85. We suspect that in the case of white-collar crime, where victims are often organizations and there are many times a number of victims of a single offense, such issues are less important. But we do not have any specific data on this question.

18. One possible explanation for the strength of this effect is simply that there are fewer federal prisons for women, and therefore what would often be a great distance between place of confinement and the local community makes imprisonment objectively more punishing for women. Beyond that, we have no special insights into this matter, but believe that, as in many other re-

The large number of consistent effects we find in examining the imprisonment decision suggests that legal critiques of the sentencing system overstate the degree of capriciousness in judicial decision making. But our model also indicates that there is disparity across the districts in the overall severity of sanctions given to white-collar offenders.[19] Those in Maryland, Northern Illinois, and Northern Texas had the greatest likelihood of imprisonment, once characteristics of offense and offender were taken into account. Those in Northern Georgia and Southern New York were least likely to go to prison. While some would argue that intercourt variability in sentencing is a legitimate reflection of the different normative climates found in different judicial districts, from the perspective of the defendants who come before the court and indeed the judicial system as a whole, inconsistency in the sentencing of different courts may be perceived as capriciousness in the sanctions received by individual defendants.

Finally, the statutory offense for which a defendant is convicted plays an important and statistically significant role in predicting imprisonment, even after we control for a wide range of other variables. An average defendant convicted of a tax violation or securities fraud faces about a two-thirds chance of a prison sentence, while a similar defendant convicted of antitrust violations or bribery has less than a one-third probability of prison.

---

spects, the answer lies deep in the history of sex-role relationships in American society. One begins with major differences in the rate of arrest by sex, which are extended through larger differentials in the rate of incarceration (see Simon, *Women and Crime* [Lexington: Lexington Books, 1975]). There is something about the specter of women behind bars and walls of the prison that leads many judges to a kind of protective paternalism. A protective response is understandable in the face of traditional cultural stereotypes of women as soft, vulnerable, "the weaker sex," and of prisons as cold, harsh, forbidding environments. In short, women are deprived of their rightful place in the masculine setting of the prison, just as they have been deprived of their rightful place in the male-dominated world of business executives (Stanton Wheeler, David Weisburd, and Nancy Bode, "Sentencing the White-Collar Offender: Rhetoric and Reality," *American Sociological Review* 47 [October 1982]:641–59, esp. 656).

19. A number of other scholars have also identified significant differences between districts in the nature of the sanctions imposed. See, for example, John Hagan, Ilene Nagel-Bernstein, and Celesta Albonetti, "The Differential Sentencing of White-Collar Offenders in Ten Federal District Courts," *American Sociological Review* 45 (1980):802–20.

How may we understand such a result? Our finding is not explained by the different statutory maximum penalties attached to individual offenses, since we have already controlled for this. One source of these differences might be the role played by independent enforcement agencies like the IRS and the SEC. By the time the cases are ready for sentencing they have been through a refined regulatory process that may winnow out most of those deserving of sanctions weaker than incarceration. But this does not help us to understand the small number incarcerated in antitrust cases, where the antitrust division of the Justice Department acts as a regulatory agency. Perhaps it is that antitrust crimes are not common-law crimes and are thus not seen as serious transgressions, despite legislative efforts. Indeed, in many countries they are not crimes at all. Taking a different tack, Michael Levi suggests that the punishment of offenders on whom others depend for work may be seen as unfairly harmful to these employees.[20] These are, of course, matters we can only speculate about. What is clear is that the statutory category itself reflects something not otherwise captured by our other indicators.

Understanding the Length of Prison Sanctions Imposed

When we examine the amount of time defendants were sentenced to serve in prison (table 6.5), we again find that factors reflecting harm and blameworthiness are important in explaining the decisions of judges.[21] Indeed, dollar victimization and maximum exposure to prison are more powerful predictors here than in the earlier model,[22]

20. Michael Levi, "Fraudulent Justice? Sentencing the Business Criminal," in *Paying for Crime,* Pat Carlen and Dee Cook, eds. (Philadelphia: Open University Press, 1989), 98.

21. Because of the discrete nature of sentencing decisions, the natural log of prison length was used as the response variable rather than the actual distribution of sentences. This served to pull the longest sentences closer to those of six or twelve months, better approximating the actual intervals of the decision the judges make. This strategy was supported by an examination of the residual scatterplot with both the actual and logged scores. In the former case, errors in prediction increase in a curvilinear fashion as the response variable gets larger. This problem disappears for the most part with the natural log solution.

22. Though it is difficult to compare the significance of these coefficients to those in the logit regression because of the reduced number of cases, it is possible to assess the relative strength of variables. When the dependent

and type of victim becomes statistically significant. At the same time the overall complexity of the offense and its geographic spread are not significant.

Assessments of blameworthiness, important in the likelihood of imprisonment analysis, generally increase in strength in this model. The respectability measure is also more important in determining the length of imprisonment than it is in predicting the probability of imprisonment. Social status, on the other hand, declines in importance and becomes statistically insignificant. Thus, the paradox of leniency and severity appears to be less important in determining sentence length than in the decision whether or not to imprison a defendant in the first place.

What of our other measures assessing the blameworthiness of defendants? In the model examining the imprisonment decision an expression of remorse decreases a defendant's probability of going to jail, but not to a statistically significant degree. Its importance grows in the model for length of sentence, and it attains statistical significance.[23] Type of plea also grows in importance and just achieves the threshold of statistical significance. Whether or not the defendant cooperated with the authorities has a small and insignificant influence upon this sentencing decision.

Again, we find little support for the discrimination model. Social class has a significant influence upon length of sentence, but its effect appears to reflect concerns of blameworthiness rather than discrimination. Those of higher class position—managers and owners—receive the longer sentences. Employees without managerial responsibilities receive the lightest sanctions. Given our other findings, we suspect that judges are assessing blameworthiness based on power and authority in the workplace.

---

variable is logged, as is the case here, unstandardized regression coefficients are approximately equal to the percent increase in the dependent variable per unit increase in the describing variable, though this relationship becomes suspect when b exceeds 0.25 (see Edward Tufte, *Data Analysis for Politics and Policy* [Englewood Cliffs, N.J.: Prentice-Hall, 1974]). This interpretation is particularly useful for us since the derivatives at mean $(0.46(1-0.46)b_n)$ in the logit regression have this same interpretation.

23. This finding appears to contradict John Braithwaite's argument that repentance is not rewarded within the American criminal justice system (*Crime, Shame and Reintegration* [New York: Cambridge University Press, 1989], 164–65).

Table 6.5. Model of the Logged Length of Imprisonment for White-Collar Offenders

Independent Variables	Coefficient
Intercept	0.916
Lambda	−0.004
From the Discrimination Perspective	
Race	0.121
Sex	−0.091
Age	−0.006
Age squared	0.000
Socioeconomic Status[2]	0.004
Social Class[1]	*
Owner	0.426**
Officer	0.026
Sole Proprietor	0.006
Manager	0.452*
(Worker)	
Type of Counsel	−0.028
Education	0.029
From the Common Sociolegal Perspective	
Organizational Complexity	0.020
Spread of Illegality	0.129
Number of Victims	−0.083
Type of Victim[1]	*
Individual	0.099
Combination	0.274
Government	−0.444*
Missing/None	−0.374
(Business)	
Dollar Victimization	0.121***
Maximum Exposure to Prison	0.071***
Respectability	−0.149**
Arrests	0.048***
Most Serious Prior Conviction	0.149**
Role in Offense[1]	
Middle	−0.165
Minor	−0.364
Missing	−0.344*
(Major)	
Source of Conviction	0.257*
Socioeconomic Status[2]	0.004
Cooperation with Authorities	−0.039
Remorse	−0.284*

Table 6.5. *Continued*

Independent Variables	Coefficient
From the Chaos Perspective	
District[1]	***
Central California	−1.203***
Maryland	−0.868***
Southern New York	−1.126***
Northern Texas	0.033
Northern Illinois	−0.629**
Western Washington	−0.547*
(Northern Georgia)	
Offense[1]	
Bank Embezzlement	−0.158
Tax Fraud	−0.074
Mail Fraud	−0.029
Securities Fraud	0.218
False Claims	0.147
Bribery	0.213
Antitrust	−1.658**
(Credit Fraud)	

$F = 7.533$ $P < 0.0001$
R-Square = 0.4487
$*p < 0.05$ $**p < 0.01$ $***p < 0.001$
441 observations

[1] Where a variable is represented by a set of dummy variables, the excluded category is listed in parentheses. The overall significance of the variable is given opposite the category name. The significance of the differences between the individual dummy variables and the excluded category is given next to each dummy variable.

[2] Socioeconomic status is relevant for both the discrimination and the jurisprudential perspectives. It is used only once in calculating predicted values.

Our results also challenge models of chaos and disarray that predict widespread inconsistency in sentencing. Our model explains almost 45 percent of the variation in the length of sentence imposed. At the same time there again is substantial variation in sentencing behavior between the districts that cannot be explained by the nature of the offenses or characteristics of offenders. Indeed, the effect here is even more powerful than for the decision of whether to imprison. In Northern Georgia, where defendants are among the least likely to face prison, those who do are sent away for longer periods than in any district other than Northern Texas. The Southern District of New York remains at the lenient end of the spectrum, where it is joined by the Central District of California (centered in Los Angeles).

Finally, statutory offense just fails to achieve a statistically significant effect on the sanction imposed, although most of this impact is due to the very short sentences received by those antitrust offenders who are sentenced to prison. Bank embezzlers and tax violators also receive shorter than average sentences, while securities offenders receive on average the longest terms of imprisonment.

The Imposition of Fines

The assumption among most scholars and laypersons has been that fines play a much more important role in white-collar crime sentencing than they do in common-crime sentencing.[24] Our data do confirm the conventional wisdom, though as before we find a considerable degree of diversity within the white-collar crime category (table 6.6). While all of the antitrust violators in the seven districts are ordered to pay fines, only 15 percent of the bank embezzlers are so sentenced. Low as it is, this latter figure is more than twice that of the common-crime sample. In only one other offense category besides antitrust—bribery—are more than half of the offenders sentenced to pay a fine.

Some have argued that fines play a significant role in sentencing primarily when a prison penalty is withheld or suspended.[25] Although the defendants in our sample are more likely to receive fines if they are not imprisoned, a substantial number of those who receive a prison sentence are also ordered by the court to pay fines.[26] For example, all of those imprisoned for antitrust violations in the seven districts also receive a monetary sanction; more than half of the imprisoned bribery defendants and more than a third of tax and SEC offenders receive this combination of sanctions.

As we look at the amount of the fines imposed, what stands out

24. See Kip Schlegel, *Just Desserts for Corporate Criminals*.

25. For example, see ibid.

26. Our findings here are consistent with those reported by Sally T. Hillsman, Barry Mahoney, George F. Cole, and Bernard Auchter ("Fines as Criminal Sanctions," *National Institute of Justice: Research in Brief*, September 1987).

Table 6.6. Fine Ordered

Offense	Percent of All Offenders with Fines Ordered	Percent of Those Sentenced to Imprisonment Given Fines	Mean Fine for Those Fined	Standard Deviation of Fines	Median Fine Ordered	N[3]
Antitrust[1]	100.0%	100.0%	$9,808	$9,703	$5,750	26
Securities Fraud[2]	38.5%	37.2%	$8,180	$8,171	$5,000	65
Bribery	62.2%	53.3%	$10,463	$28,524	$3,000	82
False Claims	34.4%	15.9%	$4,635	$6,022	$2,500	157
Mail Fraud	20.3%	15.7%	$8,400	$15,587	$2,000	187
Credit Fraud	20.5%	13.9%	$2,919	$2,891	$2,000	156
Tax Fraud	47.8%	37.7%	$5,264	$7,378	$3,000	207
Bank Embezzlement	15.1%	10.2%	$1,397	$1,394	$1,000	198
All White-Collar Crimes[4]	32.9%	25.2%	$6,250	$13,446	$3,000	1,078
Common Crimes	6.0%	0.7%	$675	$838	$200	200

[1] Includes individuals in the basic sample. Nationally, 86.6% have fines ordered, and 50% of those sentenced to imprisonment have fines ordered. The mean fine is $74,869. See Appendix 1.
[2] Includes individuals in the basic sample only. Nationally, 38.8% have fines ordered, and 34.5% of those sentenced to imprisonment have fines ordered. The mean fine is $10,759.
[3] N represents the number of individuals with nonmissing information for the variable.
[4] Includes the basic sample only. See Appendix 1.

most dramatically is the relatively lenient nature of most of these penalties. The mean fine for antitrust is $9,808, that for bank embezzlement only $1,397. Whereas the average fine for white-collar defendants is again much greater than that for the common-crime sample, and these figures would be inflated in 1990 dollars, they still are relatively modest and fall far below the megasanctions that have recently been reported in the popular press. Indeed, the largest fine in our sample was only $100 thousand, and this amount was twice as large as the next most severe fine.[27]

Clearly, one reason for the relatively modest nature of the fines is the relatively modest means of most white-collar criminals sentenced in federal courts. We have seen throughout that our white-collar offenders are better described as middle-class criminals than as upper-class or elite criminals. Many have few assets at the time of sentencing, and often their debts far outstrip their means. Some have fallen from elite positions, but most were middle or upper-middle class even at the outset. Some were professionals or white-collar workers who never attained very much. One bribery offender, for example, who had a bachelors degree in business administration and worked as a loan officer, was sentenced to thirty days confinement, a $2,500 fine and 1,200 hours of community service. He was reported to have only $700 in assets ($400 in liabilities) and an income of $800 a month. Clearly, this offender's fine was of consequence to him, even though it was relatively modest.

While the middle-class nature of white-collar criminals provides one answer for the modest size of the fines imposed, such leniency does not explain why many wealthy offenders also receive modest fines. For example, one antitrust violator received a $3,500 fine for fixing the price of certain candy bars in an eastern state. The defendant, a forty-five-year-old white male, had a net worth at time of sentencing of more than $190 thousand. Another well-off defendant, convicted of credit fraud, had a net worth of almost $1.4 million, but he received a fine of only $5 thousand. Of course, the statutory maximums themselves were often low, especially when only one count was charged.[28] But even taking into account this fact, only 4

27. A $200 thousand fine was, however, imposed on one of the codefendants we examined.

28. See Appendix 3.

percent of our offenders are ordered to pay the maximum penalty that their charges allow.

Identifying Factors that Lead to the Imposition of Fines

As a sentencing decision, the imposition of fines is conceptually more complex to model than the imposition of a prison sentence. Fines are viewed by judges as a lesser punishment,[29] and often as an alternative to prison. To adjust our earlier sentencing model to the problem of fines, we add a variable indicating whether a defendant was sentenced to imprisonment and a measure of net worth. We also replace maximum exposure to imprisonment with maximum exposure to fines. We again look only at our white-collar criminals.

Given that judges say they begin with the question of imprisonment when deliberating on sentencing, it is not surprising that the absence of a prison sanction itself is by far the single most important predictor of the imposition of a fine (table 6.7).[30] Yet, we find little else that is consistent with any of the sentencing models described above. Indeed, our results are in some ways counter to what we have already learned and lead to the conclusion that the relatively ignored problem of criminal fines should be the subject of more careful study.

29. Some theoreticians using economic models of sentencing, including Richard Posner ("Optimal Sentences for White-Collar Criminals," *American Criminal Law Review* 17 [1980]:409), have argued that this is not necessarily the case. Posner states that for every offender there is a large enough fine that the punishment would "feel" as harsh as a prison sentence. See also John Coffee, "Corporate Crime and Punishment: A Non-Chicago View of the Economics of Criminal Sanctions," *American Criminal Law Review* 17 (1980): 419; and Gary Becker, "Crime and Punishment: An Economic Approach," *Journal of Political Economy* 76 (1968):169.

30. Separate analyses (correcting for selection bias) of those who received an imprisonment sanction and those who did not show relatively small differences from the effects listed in table 6.7. The largest changes were a significant negative effect of maximum fine for those imprisoned (and an insignificant effect for others), a much larger positive effect for those who cooperated with the authorities and were sentenced to prison, and a finding that major figures in an offense sentenced to prison were less likely than others to receive a fine (but more likely if they were not sentenced to prison). The direction of these changes suggests to us that there is some element related to imprisonment not captured by our in/out measure which is influencing these models. Overall we believe that our analyses here are only a first step. We hope others will be able to examine these issues in much more detail than we were able to.

Table 6.7. Logistic Regression Model of the Probability of Being Fined, for Convicted White-Collar Offenders

Independent Variables	Coefficient	Derivative at Mean
Intercept	−2.424**	−0.530
From the Discrimination Perspective		
Race	−0.527*	−0.115
Sex	0.122	0.027
Age	0.019*	0.004
Social Class[1]	***	
Manager	0.009	0.002
Owner	1.047***	0.229
Officer	−0.141	−0.031
Sole Proprietor	−0.050	−0.011
(Worker)		
Type of Counsel	−0.835***	−0.183
Net Worth	0.000	0.000
Education	0.058	0.013
From the Common Socio-legal Norms Perspective		
In/Out	−1.034***	0.226
Organizational Complexity	0.044	0.010
Spread of Illegality	−0.018	0.004
Number of Victims	0.075	0.016
Type of Victim[1]	*	
Individual	−0.156	0.034
Combination	0.545	0.119
Government	1.039**	0.227
Missing/None	0.934*	0.204
(Business)		
Dollar Victimization	−0.006	−0.001
Maximum Fine	−0.005*	−0.001
Respectability	0.338***	0.074
Arrests	0.037	0.008
Most Serious Prior Conviction	−0.287*	−0.063
Role in the Offense[1]		
Middle	−0.718	−0.157
Minor	0.030	0.007
Missing	0.185	0.040
(Major)		
Source of Conviction	−0.003	−0.001
Remorse	0.074	0.016
Cooperation with Authorities	0.401	0.088

Table 6.7. *Continued*

Independent Variables	Coefficient	Derivative at Mean
From the Chaos Perspective		
District[1]	***	
Central California	1.202***	0.263
Maryland	0.253	0.055
Southern New York	−0.253	−0.055
Northern Texas	−0.204	−0.045
Northern Illinois	−1.179**	−0.258
Western Washington	−0.214	0.047
(Northern Georgia)		
Offense[1]	***	
Bank Embezzlement	0.710	0.155
Tax Fraud	0.815*	0.178
Mail Fraud	0.316	0.069
Securities Fraud	−0.289	−0.063
False Claims	0.634	0.139
Bribery	1.282**	0.281
Antitrust	10.379	2.269
(Credit Fraud)		

963 observations
−2 Log-Likelihood = 820.76   P < 0.001
Model Chi-Square = 390.83 with 42 Degrees of Freedom
*p < 0.05   **p < 0.01   ***p < 0.001

[1]For variables represented by a set of dummy variables, the excluded category is listed in parentheses. The overall significance of the variable is given opposite the name of the variable. The significance of the differences between the individual dummy variables and the excluded category is given next to the dummy variable.

Of our seriousness measures, only maximum fine has a statistically significant effect. Contrary to what we would expect, those convicted of crimes with higher statutory maximums are less likely to receive a fine. We suspect this result is confounded by the fact that more serious crimes are subject to higher maximum penalties. Type of victim is a significant factor in our model, although its effect is not in the predicted direction. Those who victimize the government are most likely to receive a fine.

Blameworthiness plays an important role in predicting fines, but those less blameworthy according to judges receive harsher sanctions. For example, those who have less serious prior records are more likely to be fined. Although status is not an important factor in predicting imposition of a fine, respectability is significant, with those with more stable social records more likely to receive this penalty.

Our results also run counter to models that emphasize discrimination and class bias. Those who are white, all else being equal, are more likely to be fined. Fines are also more likely to be imposed on older defendants and those represented by private attorneys. Finally, class is statistically significant, with owners the most likely to receive fines.

As earlier, we find inconsistent sentencing between districts, as well as significant disparity in sentencing between offenses. Those who commit antitrust offenses are by far the most likely to receive fines. Given this fact, we were surprised to find that SEC violators are the least likely to receive a monetary sanction, even after we had accounted for their higher rates of imprisonment.

Overall, our analysis of the imposition of fines provides a contrast with our results concerning imprisonment.[31] Many of the characteristics that lead to more severe prison sanctions have precisely the opposite influence on fines. We cannot attribute these distinctions to the assumption that fines are an alternative to imprisonment, since our multivariate analysis already controls for this variable. Nor can we attribute our findings to the fact that judges may be using fines as an alternative to probation, since our data show that there is little relation between these two sanctions once other characteristics of offense and offender have been taken into account.[32]

31. We do considerably less well in modeling the amount of fine imposed than in predicting the presence of a fine (R squared = 0.349). Few factors consistently predict judicial behavior in that model. By far the most important of these are net worth and age, with older defendants and those with greater assets receiving the largest fines. Those who victimize more than one kind of victim and those for whom the victim is difficult to identify receive harsher fines. Of lesser importance, but still statistically significant at the 0.05 level, are the in/out decision, organizational complexity, and the statutory category of the offense. More complex crimes lead to harsher fines. Bank embezzlers, antitrust violators, and those convicted of mail fraud are all more likely to receive larger fines than other white-collar criminals. Those sentenced to imprisonment also receive the larger fines.

32. When we include probation in our model it does not have a significant impact on the probability of a fine or the amount imposed.

What then can we say about our results? Judges in our sample appear to assess fines through stereotypes of those who are most likely to be able to pay.[33] Those high up the social ladder are the most likely to be fined. But irrespective of their actual ability to pay (as reflected in their net worth), white defendants, those with more impeccable records, and those who have higher class positions are more likely to be fined. It seems as though stereotypes that generally work to the benefit of these groups are, in the special circumstances of the imposition of fines, working against them.

Probation, Restitution, and Special Penalties

In addition to imprisonment and fines, judges may use other types of sanctions in criminal sentencing. They may impose state supervision through probation. They may order a defendant to make restitution to victims. Or they may sanction defendants to some type of "special penalty," such as community service or restrictions on work or movement, or to conditions attached to incarceration that allow defendants to continue some aspect of their ordinary routines. These latter penalties are strongly associated with white-collar-crime sentencing in the popular literature.

While the role and effectiveness of probation have been an important subject of research, we can say very little about probation as a sentencing decision. But two findings emerge when we examine the distribution of probation penalties (table 6.8). First, white-collar offenders are a little more likely than our comparison common-crime offenders to receive probation. In six of the eight white-collar-crime categories a larger percentage of defendants receive probation than for common crimes. Second, the ordering from least to most probation in the sample bears a fairly high correspondence to the hierarchy of white-collar crime introduced in chapters 2 and 3, with antitrust and securities-fraud offenders least likely and bank embezzlers most likely to be sentenced to probation.

33. Although we interpret our results in a different way, they are generally in line with what other studies of criminal fines have found. Sally Hillsman et al., "Fines as Criminal Sanctions." See also Sally T. Hillsman, Joyce L. Sichel, and Barry Mahoney, *Fines in Sentencing: A Study of the Use of the Fine as a Criminal Sanction* (Washington, D.C.: National Institute of Justice, 1984).

Table 6.8. Sentenced to Probation

Offense	Percent Sentenced to Probation	Mean Length of Probation (Months)	Standard Deviation of Probation	Median Probation (Months)	N[2]
Antitrust[1]	50.0%	18.5	9.3	12	26
Securities Fraud[1]	63.1%	35.3	16.5	36	65
Bribery	81.7%	32.3	16.5	30	82
False Claims	82.8%	38.1	17.3	36	157
Mail Fraud	74.9%	39.8	16.0	36	187
Credit Fraud	83.0%	36.9	18.9	36	153
Tax Fraud	79.6%	32.9	18.6	32	206
Bank Embezzlement	90.8%	34.8	15.0	36	196
All White-Collar Crimes[3]	80.2%	35.6	17.2	36	1,072
Common Crimes	69.7%	38.2	16.3	36	208

[1] Includes individuals in the basic sample. The national figures are virtually identical.

[2] N represents the number of individuals with nonmissing information for the variable.

[3] Includes the basic sample only. See Appendix 1.

Restitution provides a picture in some ways similar and in some ways different from that found for other sanctions (table 6.9). As with probation, our most elite white-collar crimes—securities violations and antitrust offenses—anchor the bottom of the distribution.[34] The least complex crime with the least victimization—bank embezzlement—lies at the top. Even here only a quarter of the defendants were ordered to make restitution, and this figure is twice as large as that for any of our other crime categories. In this our common-crime sample does not, on average, appear very different from the white-collar-crime sample.

These data appear to lead to two general conclusions. First, in crimes such as bribery or antitrust, where it is difficult to identify specific victims, the court is unlikely to order restitution. It also

34. This may be due in part to the fact that both SEC and antitrust offenders are likely to be the subject of civil penalties, and thus restitution imposed by the court becomes less important. See Levi, "Fraudulent Justice?"

Table 6.9. Payment of Restitution Ordered

Offense	Percent Ordered to Pay Restitution	N^2
Antitrust[1]	0.0%	27
Securities Fraud[1]	1.5%	65
Bribery	0.0%	84
False Claims	13.4%	157
Mail Fraud	10.0%	189
Credit Fraud	14.7%	157
Tax Fraud	9.1%	210
Bank Embezzlement	25.4%	201
All White-Collar Crimes[3]	12.3%	1,090
Common Crimes	13.3%	60

[1] Includes individuals in the basic sample. The national figures are similar.

[2] N represents the number of individuals with nonmissing information for the variable.

[3] Includes the basic sample only. See Appendix 1.

appears that restitution is more likely for those crimes where the harm is relatively small.[35]

A number of scholars and laypeople have argued that "special penalties" are used by judges as a means of keeping white-collar criminals away from more traditional, and harsher, criminal sanctions.[36] While we have already established that those more advantaged in the social hierarchy do not appear to benefit at the time of sentencing, it is clear that those sanctioned under white-collar-crime

35. There is a significant negative correlation between dollar victimization and restitution.

36. See, for example, Alan L. Otten, "Mounting Charges of Leniency, Unfairness Hobble Advocates of Non-Jail Sentences," *Wall Street Journal,* October 30, 1985, 31; Jon Nordheimer, "In Lieu of Jail, Posner Must Aid Poor in Florida," *New York Times,* February 13, 1988, 1; Bryan Burrough, "The Embezzler David L. Miller Stole from His Employers and Isn't in Prison; Found Out, Executive Vowed Restitution and Moved on to New Jobs, New Victims," *Wall Street Journal,* September 19, 1986.

statutes are more likely to be given special penalties than our comparison common criminals (table 6.10). Indeed, with the exception of work release, our common criminals seldom receive any specific special penalty.

Although overall there is comparatively little variation in the absolute number of defendants in each white-collar-crime category who receive some form of special penalty, certain types of penalties are much more likely to be imposed on those convicted of particular crimes. For example, securities violators and to a lesser extent false-claims offenders are the only criminals in our sample who are sanctioned with occupational restraints. Interestingly, only one antitrust violator in our seven-district sample is sentenced to volunteer work in the community.

Examples of these penalties give some sense of the latitude that judges have in imposing special sanctions. One securities violator was ordered not to "participate or assist in the promotion of securities in any company other than —— corporation [owned by his wife] as it is presently constituted." The defendant was also told not to travel outside the continental United States. A bank embezzler was sentenced to two years probation and "directed to dispose of his automobile and pay the proceeds remaining after purchasing a lower price car over to the probation office as restitution." The sentence also noted that the "shares in the defendant's cooperative apartment used as bail security are to be surrendered as restitution."

In a number of cases, the judge ordered offenders to "improve" their financial skills and, in others, to get psychiatric help. For example, one person was "required to file a chapter 13 wage earner petition with the federal bankruptcy [court] and carry through with the terms of the wage earner plan approved by the bankruptcy court." She was also told "not to have either credit cards or a checking account" without approval of her probation officer and was ordered "to participate in a financial counseling program to be approved." In one case an offender was even ordered "to attend adult education classes at the direction of the probation officer in order to become literate."

Special penalties are used both for those who lie at the lower ranges of position and status and for those higher up. Overall, probation officers and the courts seem to place white-collar offenders in a category distinct from that of more traditional criminals. For exam-

Table 6.10. Sentenced to "Special Penalties"

Offense	Percent Required to Do Volunteer Work	Percent Required to Get Financial Planning Help	Percent Barred from an Occupation	Percent Given Work Release	Percent Given Another Special Penalty[3]	Total Percent Given Special Penalties[5]	N[2]
Antitrust[1]	3.7%	0.0%	0.1%	0.0%	11.1%	14.8%	27
Securities Fraud[1]	6.2%	0.0%	4.6%	0.0%	20.0%	30.8%	65
Bribery	8.3%	0.0%	0.0%	0.0%	12.9%	20.2%	84
False Claims	3.2%	0.6%	1.3%	3.2%	7.0%	14.6%	157
Mail Fraud	3.7%	0.5%	0.5%	0.5%	6.9%	11.6%	189
Credit Fraud	8.9%	0.6%	0.0%	4.5%	7.0%	19.1%	157
Tax Fraud	2.9%	0.0%	0.0%	6.2%	9.0%	18.1%	210
Bank Embezzlement	3.0%	0.5%	0.0%	3.0%	6.2%	13.4%	201
All White-Collar Crimes[4]	4.7%	0.4%	0.5%	3.5%	7.6%	16.5%	1,090
Common Crimes	0.7%	0.0%	0.0%	2.0%	6.7%	9.4%	210

[1]Includes individuals in the seven sample districts only. The national figures are similar.

[2]N represents the number of individuals with nonmissing information for the variable.

[3]Including being sentenced to unsupervised probation, recommended for a prison camp allowed to serve confinement on weekends, or to serve confinement at a later time. These are rare in our sample.

[4]Includes the basic sample only. See Appendix 1.

[5]Because some members of the sample received more than one special penalty the total is less than the sum of the categories.

ple, an embezzler was sentenced to work release and psychiatric care. His probation officer explained.

> Normally an offense as serious as this one would automatically receive a recommendation of incarceration. However this defendant is not regarded as one who is criminally oriented. It appears that the instant offense is a result of either gross misjudgment or a totally immature response to the situation in which the money became available, or both. Therefore, it is recommended that the defendant be sentenced to 6 months work release . . . and that he be required to seek outpatient psychiatric care at his own expense. He will be released from psychiatric care when his probation officer and psychiatrist agree that this is feasible.

Comparing White-Collar and Common-Crime Sentencing

We can now return to the problem of differences between white-collar- and common-crime sentencing. We have already established that within white-collar-crime categories those lower down the social hierarchy are not at a disadvantage when they come before the bench for judgment. The small number of cases in our common-crime sample limits our ability to generalize about common-crime sentencing, and does not allow us to go beyond an analysis of who goes to prison.[37] Nonetheless, as table 6.11 illustrates, judges appear to weight criteria for sentencing defendants in common-crime cases differently from criteria for sentencing those convicted of white-collar crimes.[38]

Most of the more important factors in common-crime sentencing are related to attributes of the defendants or of the legal process, though organizational complexity, type of victim (with individual victimization punished most harshly), and spread of illegality are

37. In the case of imprisonment only 69 cases would be included in our analysis. In turn, as only 6 percent of common criminals in our sample were sentenced to a fine there is very little variability for us to explain in a multivariate model.

38. There were large numbers of missing values for organizational complexity, spread of illegality, most serious prior offense, number of victims, and dollar victimization. Because of the relatively small number of cases in the analyses, missing values were allocated to the median categories.

stronger in this model than in the white-collar-crime model. Cooperation with authorities and remorse, while not significant in the white-
collar-crime model of the likelihood of imprisonment, are very important in explaining common-crime sentencing. Not unexpectedly, prior
record is a major factor in sentencing, with those with more serious
prior convictions much more likely to be sentenced to imprisonment.
Finally, age (with younger and older defendants receiving an even
larger break) and sex (again with women less likely to be imprisoned)
are strong and significant predictors of a prison sentence.

What does this mean in terms of our comparison of white-collar
and common-crime sentencing? First, the results support our decision to examine white-collar and common criminals separately. The
differences in the factors that influence judges in white-collar- and
common-crime cases make it unreliable to analyze both samples in
one regression model.[39] Second, judges pay more attention to attributes of offenders and the ways they present themselves in the
legal process in the case of common crimes.

Because their crimes and backgrounds are so varied, it is difficult
to establish whether common criminals overall are at a disadvantage
at the time of sentencing. However, we suspect that they would
benefit greatly if white-collar-crime sentencing criteria were applied
to them.[40] At the risk of oversimplification, common-crime offenders
have committed less serious crimes than white-collar offenders, but
their backgrounds, particularly their criminal records, are much
more damaging. Since judges emphasize the offense much more than
the offender in white-collar-crime sentencing, application of the same
standards to common-crime offenders would give them an advantage.
The sources of these differing approaches are unclear, and it may be
too simple to attribute them to simple and direct discrimination. It

39. The only way to do this would be to create interaction terms between
type of crime (i.e., white collar or common) and all variables that show significantly variant effects. To do so in this case would have resulted in a break-
down of the models due to multicollinearity.

40. To test this proposition we took the average common criminal in our
sample and calculated his predicted probability of imprisonment under the
white-collar-crime model. While such an offender has a 43 percent probability
of imprisonment in the common-crime sample, his predicted probability falls
to 13 percent in the white-collar-crime sample. While the same procedure in
reverse for the average white-collar offender also reduces his probability of
imprisonment, for him the difference is only 12 percent.

Table 6.11. Logistic Regression Model of the Probability of Imprisonment for Common-Crime Offenders

Independent Variables	Coefficients	Derivative at Mean
Intercept	−11.09***	−2.772
From the Discrimination Perspective		
Race	−0.27	−0.067
Sex	−1.23*	−0.307
Age	0.29*	0.072
Age squared	−0.00*	0.000
Social Class		
Unemployed	0.68	0.170
Type of Counsel	−0.58*	−0.145
Education	−0.06	−0.015
From the Shared Sociolegal Norms Perspective		
Organizational Complexity	0.36*	0.090
Spread of Illegality	0.74**	0.185
Number of Victims	0.25	0.062
Type of Victim[1]	**	
Individual	1.90***	0.475
Combination	1.17	0.292
Government	0.96	0.240
(Business)		
Dollar Victimization	0.16	0.040
Maximum Exposure to Prison	0.07	0.017
Respectability	−0.08	−0.020
Arrests	0.02	0.005
Most Serious Prior Conviction	0.61**	0.152
Role in the Offense[1]		
Middle	3.42	0.855
Minor	−0.40	−0.100
Missing	−0.06	−0.015
(Major)		
Source of Conviction	0.53	0.132
Remorse	−1.13*	−0.282
Cooperation with Authorities	−1.28*	−0.320
From the Chaos Perspective		
District[1]		
Central California	−0.27	−0.067
Maryland	−0.76	−0.190
Southern New York	−1.34	−0.335

Table 6.11. *Continued*

Independent Variables	Coefficients	Derivative at Mean
Northern Texas	−0.12	−0.030
Northern Illinois	−0.40	−0.100
Western Washington	0.10	0.025
(Northern Georgia)		

197 Observations
−2 Log-Likelihood = 199.35.
Model Chi-square = 73.13 with 30 Degrees of Freedom
*p < 0.05   **p < 0.01   ***p < 0.001

[1]For variables represented by a set of dummy variables, the excluded category is listed in parentheses. The overall significance of the variable is given opposite the name of the variable. The significance of differences between the individual dummy variables and the excluded category is given next to the dummy variable.

may be that, because the crimes of common-crime offenders are fairly similar to each other, judges focus on the backgrounds of individuals in order to distinguish among defendants. Similarly, because the criminal backgrounds of white-collar offenders are relatively homogeneous, judges may rely upon characteristics of offenses to differentiate among them. Our findings thus answer one set of questions, but raise another, which would have to be addressed with a very different type of research project.

Additional Methodological Concerns

Before concluding this chapter we want to address two issues that could be raised to challenge our general conclusions. The first, the question of sample selection bias, relates to our findings regarding socioeconomic-status and class effects upon sentencing, in particular upon the judicial decisions about imprisonment and length of confinement. The second, that of how much variation in sentencing we have really explained, may be raised about any of our multivariate models and is a common problem in social science research.

In chapter 1 we discussed the fact that generalizations based upon our sample must be tempered by the reality of a criminal-justice system in which a relatively small number of offenders reach the stage of sentencing. The dark figure of crime is particularly difficult to assess in white-collar crime, though we did point out that there are many reasons to believe that our defendants provide a fairly good sampling of those who begin the criminal process. But we noted then and repeat now that a sample of convicted offenders is not the same as a sample of all those who commit crimes. While we find little evidence of bias and discrimination at the time of the sentencing of convicted white-collar defendants, such biases may be operating in the processes that lead from detection to conviction. About the biases that precede the conviction stage we can say little or nothing.

Recently, the National Academy of Sciences (NAS) Panel on Sentencing Research has raised a slightly different problem, which is important in light of our finding that higher social and economic position often work against defendants at time of sentencing:

> Sample selection can also pose serious threats to the validity of statistical results even within the selected sample. In the case of sentencing, internal selection biases can arise when unobserved and thus unmeasured factors are common to both the selection and sentence processes, thereby inducing (or altering) correlations in the selected samples between the unmeasured variables and other included variables that are also common to selection and sentencing.[41]

In particular, the NAS Panel was concerned that errors in assessing the seriousness of crimes might hide class or race effects, this because defendants who are white or of higher status may also commit more serious offenses. If any aspect of seriousness is neglected, for example, through information available to the judge but not documented in the PSIS, then it might appear in statistical analyses that white defendants or those of higher status are being treated more harshly though they have in fact committed more harmful offenses.

We have paid particular attention to modeling aspects of offense

41. Alfred Blumstein, Jacqueline Cohen, Susan Martin, and Michael H. Tonroy (National Research Council Panel on Sentencing Research), eds., *Research on Sentencing: The Search for Reform* (Washington: National Academy Press, 1983), vol. 1, p. 103. See also the chapter by Klepper in vol. 2.

behavior and offender background that are consistent with the ways in which judges sentence white-collar-crime defendants. Moreover, for most of our sample the presentence investigations themselves provide the primary source of offense and offender information for judges. For these reasons, and because our findings of status and class effects are strong and consistent, we suspect that a correction for sample selection bias would not appreciably alter our results. Nonetheless, it is clear that our models would have been much stronger had we been able to include information on those who were filtered out of sentencing at earlier stages. Our problem here, and that of other researchers as well, is that it is virtually impossible to take into account all of the various selection processes that operate in the criminal-justice system—from the decision to investigate, to the decision to take legal action, to the decision to prosecute under criminal statutes, to the decisions that occur in bargaining over conviction.[42]

The second question relates to how well our models predict sentencing behavior. In our study, as in most others, most of the variance in sentencing remains unexplained. We have no doubt that an important part of this unexplained variation in sentencing reflects variations in sentencing practices among judges. This variation is not inconsistent with the model of common sociolegal norms we believe best fits our data. Indeed, Wheeler, Mann, and Sarat argue that the norms that inform white-collar-crime sentencing provide only general guidelines on the variables that should influence sentencing patterns:

> Despite there being broad agreement on the basic principles, there is little evidence that different judges employ the same methods of measuring harm, blameworthiness, and consequence, weighting these factors, or translating them into a specific disposition. In fact, it is difficult to determine just how judges combined factors in making assessments of different aspects of the same case. We suggest that there is an important difference between the task of identifying the basic factors guiding sentencing decisions, about which there is much agreement, and the task of

42. See Richard Berk, "Sample Selection in Sociological Data," *American Sociological Review* 48 (1983):386–98.

measuring, weighting, and combining those factors into a specific disposition.[43]

Our data reflect the considerable variability among judges in bringing legal norms to reality in sentencing.

It would be a mistake, however, to overemphasize the unexplained variance in our analyses of sentencing. These findings are strong, clear, and, for the most part, consistent. For criminologists who use prior research as a yardstick for how well a model is predicting, our results reflect a high degree of predictability in human behavior.

For the most significant sentencing decisions we find that judicial behavior is strongly informed by what Wheeler, Mann, and Sarat define as common sociolegal norms. Those committing more serious crimes and those more "blameworthy" are indeed receiving more severe sanctions. And this is true even when the norms judges advocate appear to contradict strongly held assumptions about the criminal-justice system—as is the case with the strong positive effect of social status upon the decision to imprison. But it is certainly possible that our results, especially as regards the relationship between social standing and sentencing, are time-bound and reflect the special character of the period we studied.

We have no doubt that the Watergate period led to increased prosecution of white-collar crime in the federal courts and some greater awareness of the seriousness of white-collar crimes and the need to punish them more harshly. Furthermore, judges today do not have the same amount of discretion as the ones we studied, because they are constrained by the federal sentencing guidelines. At the same time, we believe that the sentencing patterns we have identified are historically rooted and far antedate the events of the early 1970s.[44] Statutes providing prison terms for the violation of public

43. Wheeler, Mann, and Sarat, *Sitting in Judgment,* 168.
44. The view that the Watergate period caused a temporary increase in sentence severity for white-collar crime is supported by John Hagan and Patricia Parker in a study of securities violators in Canada ("White Collar Crime and Punishment: The Class Structure of Securities Violations," *American Sociological Review* 50 [1985]:302–16) but rejected by M. Benson and E. Walker in a study of white-collar crime modeled on our own in one midwestern

trust reach back well into the nineteenth century. Nor is the idea of heavier sanctions for those more highly placed limited to the United States or to the recent past. A wide variety of historical settings gives evidence of the relationship, including Renaissance Venice, the Roman Catholic church in medieval Europe, and England circa A.D. 1100.[45] In any event, we are persuaded that, although the phenomenon may have been enhanced by Watergate, the sentencing patterns of our judges are part of a broader cultural pattern with deep historical roots.

---

judicial district ("Sentencing the White Collar Offender," *American Sociological Review* 53 [1988]:294–302).

45. See Guido Ruggiero, *Violence in Early Renaissance Venice* (New Brunswick, N.J.: Rutgers University Press, 1980); John T. MacNeil and Helena Gamer, *Medieval Handbooks of Penance: A Translation of the Principal Libri Poenitentials and Selections from Related Documents* (New York: Columbia University Press, 1938); Morris S. Arnold, Thomas A. Green, Sally A. Scully, and Stephan D. White, *On the Laws and Customs of England: Essays in Honor of Samuel E. Thorne* (Chapel Hill: University of North Carolina Press, 1981). We are indebted to David Greenberg for the first of these citations and to John Beckerman for the third. Beckerman notes that "St. Jerome's directions for confessors, adapted by the English Church at the time of King Edgar, state 'As always, as a man is mightier, or of higher degree, so shall he the more deeply amend wrong, before God and before the world'" (in Arnold et al., 162).

7

Conclusions

The concept of white-collar crime has been fraught with ambiguity ever since its creator, Edwin H. Sutherland, first began writing about it. As it has evolved over the past fifty years, some have used it to focus on the status or occupation of the offender, and others have examined crimes that create particular forms of harm. Others have examined a set of particular crimes thought to be generally "white collar" in character, whatever their consequences or their ties to the status or the work of those who commit them.

We followed the latter course. In chapter 1 we laid out our reasons for making this choice, but as we near the end of our analysis it is time to reconsider that decision. After reviewing briefly the major themes that have emerged from our research, we want to use this chapter as an occasion to examine more closely the original decision to define white-collar crime broadly. We shall do so by exploring empirically what would have happened if we had used a much more refined concept of white-collar crime, one that stresses its class and status dimensions, instead of the broader, statute-based conception that we employed. We believe that analysis lends strong support to our original choice, and we engage in an extended speculation about the implications of this broader conception for our understanding of the nature of crime in American society, as well as the relation of this conception to current criminological theory. We close the chapter with our thoughts about the policy implications of our study.

Major Themes

White-collar crime in the federal courts is systematically different from nonviolent economic crime of a non-white-collar type. Even when we examine those crime categories "least" white collar in our own sample, there remain substantial differences between white-collar and common crime. This is true for the relatively limited comparison group forced upon us by our study of federal offenders, a group restricted to those convicted of postal theft and postal forgery, and we believe it would be even more true were the comparison with a typical group of street offenders.

Although they differ systematically from common-crime offenses, the white-collar crimes committed by those we studied have a mundane, common, everyday character. Their basic ingredients are lying, cheating, and fraud, and for every truly complicated and rarified offense there are many others that are simple and could be carried out by almost anyone who can read, write, and give an outward appearance of stability. The offenders that got the most notoriety in Sutherland's day were Ivar Krueger and Samuel Insull,[1] while today's most noted defendants are Ivan Boesky and Michael Milken. But now, just as in Sutherland's day, these cases are the exception, not the rule. If one wants to understand the full range of white-collar crime, one has to look beyond the most dramatic cases.

When we turn from offenses to offenders our results once again challenge conventional conceptions of white-collar criminality. While the white-collar crimes we examine draw from distinctively different sectors of the American population than do common crimes, our white-collar criminals are generally not those who are identified with the very highest ranges of class and status in American society. Nor are these the crimes of the underclass. Rather, as we noted in chapter 3, they appear to represent (with some exceptions) the broad middle of the society, much above the poverty line, but for the most part far from elite social position and status.

1. See Robert Shaplen, *Kreuger: Genius and Swindler* (New York: Alfred A. Knopf, 1960).

Even more than the everyday quality of many of the offenses, and of many of the offenders themselves, we are struck by the enormous diversity in white-collar criminality. The presentence investigation reports provide at least one or two examples of virtually every possible combination of offense and offender, from professionals committing the simplest of white-collar offenses to persons in the lower reaches of organizations conducting highly complex schemes—all in all, a rich variety of offenders and offending.

One way to introduce some order into that variety is through the notion of a hierarchy of white-collar offending, where those at the top of the hierarchy, as a rule, commit more complex offenses that cause great harm, compared to those whose offenses are less damaging and who come from less powerful positions in society. At the top of the hierarchy are antitrust and securities fraud, with bribery, mail fraud, and false claims and statement offenders occupying a moderate position, and tax fraud, credit fraud, and bank embezzlement offenders at the lower end of the hierarchy. Some might want to think of those at the top of the hierarchy as being the "pure" white-collar offender, with the colors of the collars shading off toward pink and blue as one moves down the hierarchy. But even at the bottom, as we have noted, the offenders and offenses differ from their common-crime counterparts.

In exploring further how the two major components of the offense and the offender fit together, we were particularly interested, as others have been, in two ingredients of the offending: First, how harmful the offense is to others, as measured by the amount of monetary loss and the nature and number of victims; and second, the degree of organizational complexity of the offending, as indicated by the commission of crimes exhibiting a pattern, of long duration, involving the use of organization, and with five or more participants in the offense. Without repeating the details here (they can be found in chapter 4), the crucial finding is that there is a systematic relationship between these two dimensions of offending. The crimes that do the greatest economic and social damage in our sample are those most organizationally complex. Organization in this sense is the weapon par excellence in the commission of the most damaging white-collar crimes.[2]

2. See also Stanton Wheeler and Mitchell Rothman, "The Organization as Weapon in White Collar Crime," *Michigan Law Review* 80 (1982):1403–26.

This finding enriches our understanding of white-collar offending because it helps clarify the relationship of the offender's background, his or her status, class, or occupational position, and the nature of the offense. To oversimplify only slightly, the social background characteristics do a lot to put persons in positions that allow the conduct of organizationally complex crimes. But it is being in such a position directly in an organization or with access to it, rather than status or background itself, that is the primary mechanism enabling the commission of the offenses of greatest victimization.

Seen against this background, the way in which one's professional position is related to white-collar offending may be seen with new appreciation. On some occasions the accountants, the physicians, and, particularly, the lawyers in our sample are in organizational positions that allow for commission of complex and, from their point of view, highly rewarding offenses. This is true, for example, of the lawyers who are officers or presidents of securities firms. Often, however, being a professional confers generally high social status but does not put one in such a position. Thus, some lawyers commit simple tax frauds unrelated to their profession, except in the narrow sense that it is the profession that enabled them to make the money they are now trying to keep from the tax authorities.

We endeavored to examine the movement of our white-collar criminals through the legal process from the point of discovery of their offenses through sentencing. Our findings here are exploratory, since the PSIs are not an ideal data source for this purpose. But as the first investigators, to our knowledge, to have these kinds of data available, we felt an obligation to learn as much as we could, despite working with documents designed for a different purpose. The details are in chapter 5. To summarize briefly, we found both some reinforcement of conventional wisdom and some findings that, if not novel, are at least intriguing. In the former category is the evidence of a very strong linkage between the nature of the offense and how it is detected. Some offenses, like bank embezzlement, depend heavily on discovery by the victim or the victimized organization, whereas others, such as tax fraud, depend on the surveillance of agencies like the IRS. Still others depend on tips from informants.

Our evidence on the relative likelihood of a defendant's providing information to prosecutors confirmed another commonly held notion. "Little fish" are much more likely to be cast in the role of cooperative witness than are "big fish," in part, presumably, because prosecutors are more willing to give benefits to those lower down in the scheme who can help convict those higher up. Some big fish, like Ivan Boesky, still cooperate because they have so much to give with respect to other related crimes and so much to gain from giving it.

In the more intriguing category is the finding that a substantial number of white-collar offenders do not have the wherewithal to afford private attorneys, and despite their generally white-collar backgrounds are dependent on the resources of the state through court-appointed attorneys or public defenders. Also in the intriguing category is the notion that, if there is a clear benefit to those who have employed a private attorney in the late stages of a case, it lies in the capacity of such attorneys to prevent their clients from going before harsher judges, rather than in getting them into the hands of a lenient judge. As we note in the chapter, the possibilities for "judge shopping" now have been reduced in the federal system, but our findings may apply to other jurisdictions.

Does going through the process itself constitute severe punishment, in the form of damage to business or employment, to self through physical or mental deterioration, or to family? We have only ambiguous and partial results. Our antitrust violators, those who often occupy the highest positions and therefore have the longest way to fall, would appear to be the most immune to the effects of criminal-justice processing. They rarely lose their jobs, and they show fewer signs of the other kinds of damage than do the remaining offenders. At the other end of the spectrum are bank embezzlers, who are most likely to lose their employment and often rank highly for other forms of suffering.

We began this project with an interest in the sentencing of white-collar offenders, and we returned to that interest in chapter 6. There we compared three generalized pictures or images of the sentencing process: a picture based on the assumption that all is chaos and disarray, a picture based on the assumption that the system is rife with discrimination and systematic bias in sentencing, and a picture based on the assumption that sentencing expresses the application of shared sociolegal principles centered on concepts of harm and blameworthiness. Although no single picture receives total confirmation, the results are much more consistent with the latter interpretation than the other two. This does not mean that sentencing cannot be improved upon, or that there are not instances of prejudice on the part of particular judges or of systematic discrimination in one or another jurisdiction. But the consistency with which indicators of harm and blameworthiness—the same indicators that judges report as important in their sentencing—are found to be significantly related to both the decision to imprison and the length of the term lends support to the model of common sociolegal principles.

On the question of discrimination, the results are a bit more complicated.[3] We find no evidence of racial disparity in our examination of prison sentences, but we do find evidence of gender disparity: Women on the average are less likely to be imprisoned than similarly situated men. In our examination of fines there was evidence of discrimination, but in general those of more advantaged position or background were more likely to be fined. Another form of possible disparity concerns differences between the federal districts. Defendants in some districts, like Northern Texas, are given harsher sentences for the same offense than those in some other districts, such as Southern New York. This may be viewed, however, either as systematic discrimination in sentencing or as a permissible variation allowing the norms of the local community to come into play. In any event, it is evident that sentencing severity is not uniform across the districts we studied.

Or at least it wasn't at the time we studied them. Our study, as we noted earlier, is specifically rooted in time and place and in the federal courts. Our results hold for sentences for selected federal crimes in seven of the major jurisdictions in the United States between 1976 and 1979.[4] Since that time administration and prosecution policy have changed in ways that might affect sentencing. Insider trading, for example, has become a high priority for the SEC during the 1980s. However, statistics about the white-collar offenses

3. We are limited in our analysis to the examination of discrimination at the final stages of the legal process. We cannot, on the basis of these data, make any generalizations about discrimination in the criminal-justice system or its specific role at any earlier stages of the legal process.

4. Benson and Walker ("Sentencing the White Collar Offender," *American Sociological Review* 53[1988]:294–302) argue that smaller districts have somewhat different sentencing patterns than those found in our study. While our concern with white-collar crime led us to federal districts which evidence relatively large numbers of white-collar prosecutions, we do not find major differences when comparing smaller and larger districts in our sample.

presently prosecuted and the number of defendants who go to prison suggest that there have not been major changes since the time of our study.[5] Accordingly, save for the observations noted in the preface, we have no reason to believe that the broad patterns we found would have changed in any dramatic way during the intervening years.

A Reevaluation of the Concept of White-Collar Crime

We think our results are solid and provide us with a new understanding of white-collar crime. But that conclusion raises a very important question that we addressed in chapter 1 and need to return to now: What justification is there for a definition or a conception of white-collar crime that does not automatically tie that conception to the status, class, or occupation of the criminal? What justification is there for including under the same general rubric a truck driver who falsifies his federal loan application and a surgeon who falsifies his income tax return? What justification is there for including in the same sample both the highly placed lawyer who runs the securities firm and the lowly placed secretary who may have played a minor but knowing role in a securities fraud scheme? What justification is there for conducting a study of white-collar individuals while ignoring the corporations that were at the core of Sutherland's original analysis?

About this last question we can do very little but acknowledge that the criminality of organizations is an important topic, indeed an increasingly important one, as recent federal legislation enables the government to attack criminal enterprise directly through statutes like RICO. In short, we are sure that there are a series of inquiries to be undertaken (some of which have already been completed)[6] that will

5. See Kathleen Daly, "Gender and Varieties of White Collar Crime," *Criminology* 27 (1989):769–93; Donald Manson, "Tracking White Collar Criminals" (Washington: Bureau of Justice Statistics, 1986).

6. See, for example, John Braithwaite, *Corporate Crime in the Pharmaceutical Industry* (London: Rutledge and Kegan Paul, 1984); Marshall Clinard and Peter Yeager, *Corporate Crime* (New York: Free Press, 1980); Diane Vaughan, *Controlling Unlawful Organizational Behavior: Social Structure and Corporate Misconduct* (Chicago: University of Chicago Press, 1983); Kip Schlegel, *Just Deserts for the Corporate Criminal* (Boston: Northeastern University Press, 1990).

shed light on organizational as distinct from individual crime, and on the organization as distinct from individual members as targets of enforcement activity. Our own interest in the organizational dimension should be clear from the extent to which we have emphasized the importance of the use of organizational complexity in the commission of white-collar crimes. But aside from occasional small-scale inquiries, we were not able to address the organizational questions directly. Our failure to do so in no way indicates lack of interest in the problem.

But the crimes of corporations and other organizations are still carried out by individuals, and it is relevant to examine those individuals in detail, as we have tried to do throughout this book. We return, therefore, to the first set of questions posed above. Our general answer is to approach the problem empirically: How much difference would it have made in our study if we had restricted our definition of white-collar offenders to a much narrower group, more closely approximating classic conceptions based on status, class, or occupation?

One of those conceptions has been spelled out by Jack Katz, when he examined differences in the prosecution of white-collar and common crime.[7] He restricts the definition of white-collar crime to include only offenders of "white collar social class" and, among that class, those who use their occupation to commit the crime. Katz raises other issues relating to the nature of the covering up of offenses, and whether the crime was made to appear as part of an office routine, that we find harder to deal with directly, but we can address these two core ingredients. By white-collar class position Katz means "bourgeois professions (doctor, lawyer, accountant, cleric), the managerial ranks of public and private corporations, public officials with significant discretionary powers (i.e., not mailmen), and owners of substantial capital."[8]

For the 1,090 defendants drawn from our seven jurisdictions, we operationalized Katz's conception of white-collar class by identifying those people who have had at least one of the common characteristics: an occupational title during the actual offense of doctor, judge, law-

7. Jack Katz, "Legality and Equality: Plea Bargaining in the Prosecution of White-Collar and Common Crime," *Law and Society Review* 13 (1979):431–59.

8. Ibid., 434.

Table 7.1. Percent of the Defendants Who Meet a Restrictive
Definition of White-Collar Criminals

Offense	Percent	N[2]
Antitrust[1]	100.0%	27
Securities Fraud[1]	72.3%	65
Bribery	47.6%	84
Mail Fraud	30.2%	189
Credit Fraud	26.8%	157
False Claims	25.5%	157
Bank Embezzlement	23.4%	201
Tax Fraud	9.1%	210
All White-Collar Crimes[3]	29.2%	1,090

[1] For the seven-district sample only. Figures for the national sample are comparable.

[2] N represents the number of individuals with nonmissing information for the variable.

[3] Includes the basic sample only. See Appendix 1.

yer, accountant, or clergyman; a social class of manager, owner, or officer; or assets of at least $500 thousand. The management class includes government managers and inspectors. Of our cases, 370 fit this definition of white-collar social class. We eliminated people who did not use their occupation to commit their offense; that left us with 319 defendants.

To get a sense for how this new definition works in comparison with our older, broader one, we show in table 7.1 an ordering of the offenses from our broader sample by the percentage of them that also fit Katz's definition. As the reader can see, all of the antitrust offenders and three-quarters of the SEC offenders are defined as white collar using the more restrictive Katz criteria, while at least a fifth of the other categories except tax fraud would meet them.

Although one could have limited our study to the examination of antitrust and securities-fraud offenders and stayed largely within this restricted definition, note how restricted the definition really is. If we think of white-collar crime as falling somewhere on a continuum between pure white-collar and pure common crime, the question is where to establish a cut-off point. We have simply drawn the line a little further away from the "pure white collar" type than some might have preferred. But if we turn the question around and ask how many

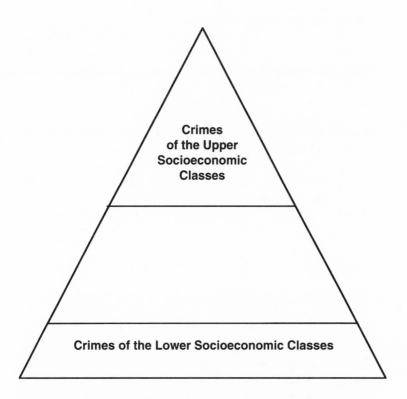

Figure 7.1. Graphic Representation of Traditional Conceptions of the Crime Problem

of our defendants have at least one or more attributes that are characteristic of white-collar crime, we get a very different feeling about the distribution. For example, 95 percent of the bank embezzlers use their occupation in the commission of their offense. And virtually everyone in our sample fits the Edelhertz definition of white-collar crime as "an illegal act or series of illegal acts committed by nonphysical means and by concealment and guile, to obtain money or property, to avoid payment or loss of money or property, or to obtain business or personal advantage."[9]

9. Herbert Edelhertz, *The Nature, Impact and Prosecution of White Collar Crime* (Washington: Department of Justice, 1970), 3.

The difference between what we will call for the moment the "traditional" approach of limiting sharply the definition of white-collar crime and our approach can be portrayed graphically (see figure 7.1). Those who would limit white-collar crime solely to the crimes of the upper classes and the corporate world, and would compare it to common crime, street crime, or the usual conception of "the crime problem," are examining the top and the bottom of the stratification system and virtually leaving out the entire middle. In so doing, they give an image of crime as a two-class system, either the top or the bottom, with little being said about the vast middle. Our conception restores that middle "class" of crime, most of which is indeed "middle" in at least some of its class attributes, to an important place in the examination of the crime problem. To leave it out is to leave out, in effect, the lower two levels of the hierarchy we have talked about earlier. By being inclusive rather than exclusive, we have been able to demonstrate empirically the relationship between varying degrees of "white collarness" and other attributes of offending, and at the same time to restore an important category to the study of crime.

Rethinking White-Collar Crime

Sutherland noted in the introductory chapter to *White Collar Crime* that studies of crime were biased toward those in the lower socioeconomic class.[10] He reproduced data from the Gluecks' studies showing that most families of delinquents are of dependent or marginal status, that they often show high rates of unemployment and low rates of formal education. He drew from census data to show the low weekly earnings of those committed to state prisons or reformatories, and he drew from the early ecological studies of the Chicago school to show the high ecological correlation between the rate of delinquency cases and the number of families on relief.[11]

10. Edwin H. Sutherland, *White Collar Crime: The Uncut Version* (New Haven: Yale University Press, 1983), 3–10.
11. Sheldon Glueck and Eleanor Glueck, *One Thousand Juvenile Delinquents* (Cambridge: Harvard University Press, 1934); Sheldon Glueck and Eleanor Glueck, *Five Hundred Criminal Careers* (New York: A. A. Knopf, 1930); Sheldon Glueck and Eleanor Glueck, *Five Hundred Delinquent Women* (New York: A. A. Knopf, 1934); United States Bureau of the Census, *The*

Sutherland also argued, indeed it is central to his thesis, that persons of the upper socioeconomic class are often processed "under laws which apply exclusively to business and the professions and which therefore involve only the upper socioeconomic class. Persons who violate laws regarding restraint of trade, advertising, pure food and drugs and similar business practices, are not arrested by uniformed policemen, are not tried in criminal courts, and are not committed to prisons; their illegal behavior receives the attention of administrative commissions and of courts operating under civil or equity jurisdiction."[12] It was largely this bias in processing that led Sutherland to examine the violations of large corporations.

In other words, having noted the preponderance of the poor and the marginal in traditional studies, and the absence of the privileged, he set out to rectify the problem by studying a group sure to contain primarily the latter. This is entirely understandable given Sutherland's mission, but what it does, in effect, is to hide from view the whole middle category. Actually, even the studies he used to illustrate his argument gave evidence of a fairly substantial proportion of offenders from backgrounds above the floor of poverty. For example, of the delinquents in two of the three studies of the Gluecks he drew upon, roughly a quarter are judged to have come from "comfortable" circumstances.[13] And 40 percent of the persons committed to state and federal prisons and reformatories in the 1923 study he cited had weekly earnings of $30 or more—not so small by the standards of the early 1920s.

But Sutherland, though he surely recognized the existence of such data, could make his point more clearly by focusing on the business and corporate people at the top of the social order, rather than on those average folks around the middle. Indeed, as Sutherland stated the primary thesis of his book, it is that "persons of the upper socio-economic class engage in much criminal behavior; that this criminal

Prisoner's Antecedents (Washington, D.C.: GPO, 1923); Clifford R. Shaw and Henry D. McKay, *Juvenile Delinquency and Urban Areas* (Chicago: University of Chicago Press, 1943).

12. Sutherland, *White Collar Crime,* 6.

13. The other study, limited to young female delinquents, has a far lower proportion. See Sutherland, *White Collar Crime,* page 4, where he cites Glueck and Glueck.

behavior differs from the criminal behavior of the lower socioeconomic class principally in the administrative procedures which are used in dealing with the offenders; and that variations in administrative procedures are not significant from the point of view of causation of crime."[14] In thus addressing crime in the upper classes and in the lower classes, and saying nothing about the middle, he treated the middle category as though it were hardly there at all.

It is also understandable that Sutherland may have failed to give attention to this category, given the structure of the society and the labor force during the time his ideas were being formed. During the 1920s and 1930s, the white-collar class as a category of labor was smaller than it is today,[15] and it is possible that not much was lost by concentrating on the crimes at the bottom and the top of the social order, and leaving out the white-collar middle. But by the latter part of the twentieth century, the postindustrial world has generated vast numbers of white-collar jobs and white-collar families. By now, if not so clearly half a century ago, the image of only two classes of offenders is misplaced, for it leaves out a large part of what may be the heart of the American population.

What our data locate, then, is a broad band of offending above the floor of crime usually associated with street crime with its base in an underclass, yet below, in some sense, the quintessential white-collar crimes and criminals that usually receive media attention and that are represented in our data primarily by the antitrust and securities-fraud offenders.

What can we say about this new category of people and their crimes? One thing is to note the availability of fraud and deceit and dishonesty, and the crimes based upon them, as the kinds of offenses that *every person* may commit. They do not take the physical skills and dexterity of many forms of street crime, or even the consummate skills of con artists like the legendary Yellow Kid Weil.[16] Many of the crimes require not much more than the ability to read, write, and fill

14. Sutherland, *White Collar Crime,* 7.

15. See Daniel Bell, *The Coming of Post-Industrial Society* (New York: Basic Books, 1973), 134–35, for a discussion of long-term changes in the makeup of the American occupational structure.

16. See "Yellow Kid" Weil, as told to W. T. Brannon, *"Yellow Kid Weil": The Autobiography of America's Master Swindler* (New York: Ziff-Davis, 1948).

out forms, along with some minimum level of presentation of a respectable self.

The conditions for the commission of these forms of crime are created in part by the credit economy. Credit cards produce credit fraud. When persons are induced to buy on credit, are encouraged to extend their lines of credit, are encouraged to run up large amounts of debt, pressure is created for more borrowing and potentially more debt. Many of the defendants in our sample were not without financial resources, but the balance between their resources and their commitments was out of whack.

We believe that ordinary people are committing white-collar crime in increasing numbers.[17] One reason is that ordinary people now have greater access to the white-collar world of paper fraud. For example, more and more men and women work with computers, a technology that barely existed forty years ago, but one that now has a permanent place in national and international life. More and more white-collar computer employees find their jobs attached to some form of banking or company finance, and the potential to cheat is great. Since the nation's financial community and its stock markets are linked by computers, there is little doubt that fraud is a major concern, but one financial leaders dislike discussing publicly.

Such conditions are also created by the programs of a welfare state. Virtually all federal programs—including HUD, Social Security, Medicaid, and other welfare programs—depend on written materials, and all have the potential for submission of fraudulent applications. Experience with such programs does not have to await middle age. Vast numbers of persons of college age now have experience with student loan programs, for example.

These changes are reinforced by the development of a society that runs on the basis of credentials.[18] When formal credentials, based upon grades, graduation, awards, and the like, become the basis for social evaluation and social status, there will be pressures to inflate the credentials, or to make them up when they do not exist. Thus, there is pressure to cheat on exams in the school system, pressure for

17. See Michael Levi, *Regulating Fraud* (New York: Tavistock, 1987), 4–10.

18. See Randall Collins, *The Credential Society: A Historical Sociology of Education and Stratification* (New York: Academic Press, 1979).

puffery in the preparation of application forms, to make one's self out to be a little (or a lot) better than the formal record might legitimately allow. Nor do these pressures cease when a person manages to get a toehold in an established institution, as the cases of research fraud in universities attest.[19]

If the efforts to achieve succeed, whether legitimately or illegitimately, the person will be able to upgrade his or her car, home, or lifestyle. The message reinforced by television values and in advertising is not to settle for second best. The continued pressure of a value system that rewards economic affluence or its visible by-products has its effects on the broad middle of American society, from those at its lower edges who may be struggling with low-paying white-collar jobs (like the bank tellers in our sample), or those in modest-paying positions in government bureaucracies, as well as those at the upper range or on their way there, whose aspirations outrun their perhaps considerable achievements, but who are not yet in the privileged positions of power and trust that we associate with the original conception of white-collar crime.

These are, in other words, typical Americans using the ubiquitous weapon of dishonesty to commit crimes. We all understand that some answers on forms are more likely to bring forth money or benefits than are other answers. In this sense, lying and cheating are truly the weapons available to us all, and the IRS form, the phony invoice, the fraudulent application, or the hidden agreement that leads to mutual though illegal advantage are mechanisms for the commission of a virtually limitless number of crimes. Collusion has the added requirement of someone to collude with, and it is present in many of our white-collar offenses. But there are many that can be committed on one's own, with nothing more than the will to deceive.

From this point of view, then, the people we studied are the core American criminals, whose ranks will grow as the society becomes ever more middle class, as credit cards and credentialing grow, as television continues to hammer home the message of consumption. These are not the people who make the streets feel unsafe and who

19. David Stipp, "Competition in Science Seems to Be Spawning Cases of Bad Research: Plagiarism and Data Faking Mar Field that Needs Trust," *Wall Street Journal,* July 12, 1985. For an example of a specific case, see Janny Scott, "Researcher Admits Faking Data to Get $160,000 in Funds," *Los Angeles Times,* September 20, 1988.

keep others from going out at night. Their crimes are not like the crimes of underclass street criminals, characterized by violence and threats to physical safety. But they are also not like the stereotype of the rich and powerful white-collar offender at the pinnacle of society. Rather, they primarily resemble the broad middle of American society, above the poverty line by varying degrees and anxious to climb closer to the top. Some members of this broad-based group have access to the organizational resources required to commit the most substantial crimes, whereas others do not. Whether or not such resources are used, the skills required for most of these crimes are minimal, and many of the crimes seem mundane. Yet this is also why we believe that these are in many ways the prototypical American forms of crime.

Middle-Class Criminals in Relation to Contemporary Criminological Theory

Among criminologists, the concept of white-collar crime has long played an important role in challenging conventional theory. As we noted in earlier chapters, Sutherland used his research on white-collar criminality to refute the predominant concern in his day with poverty and social disorganization in the development of deviant behavior. Today, white-collar crime has once more emerged as an important part of criminological debate.[20] In this case, though, the controversy does not center around a particular theory in criminology but on whether crime as such may be understood with reference to a single explanatory system.[21] We do not want to close our discussion without examining how our analyses may contribute to this debate.

Is white-collar crime a special phenomenon requiring an explana-

20. See Travis Hirschi and Michael Gottfredson, "Causes of White Collar Crime," *Criminology* 25 (1987):949–74; Darrell Steffensmeier "——— Crime: An assessment of Hirschi and Gottfredson's claims," *Criminology* 27 (1989):345–58; Travis Hirschi and Michael Gottfredson, "The Significance of White Collar Crime for a General Theory of Crime," *Criminology* 27 (1989): 369–71.

21. See Steffensmeier, "——— Crime"; David Weisburd, Lisa Maher, and Lawrence Sherman, "Contrasting Crime General and Crime Specific Theory: The Case of Hot Spots of Crime," in *Advances in Criminological Theory* 4 (1993):45–70.

tion different from that required of common crime? More specifically, with respect to our own findings, do the crimes occurring at different levels in the hierarchy of white-collar criminality each require a separate explanation? If Ronald Clarke and Derek Cornish are correct then here, as for other types of crime, the more specific our explanations become the more they will explain and the more useful our theorizing will be.[22]

But Travis Hirschi and Michael Gottfredson come to a very different conclusion when they examine the distribution of white-collar crime as reported in official statistics, a conclusion that they believe supports their more general view that "crime is a unitary phenomenon capable of explanation by a single theory."[23] They believe that the category of white-collar crime itself has served more to confuse debate about the origins of criminality than to clarify and develop such theory, and thus they attack the value of white-collar crime as a concept. They argue that their data, as well as our finding of the mundane everyday character of white-collar crime and criminals, suggest that the distinctions between white-collar and common crime are for the most part (at least in terms of their source and motivation) trivial.[24]

The general thrust of the theory of crime that Hirschi and Gottfredson present is, interestingly enough, quite similar in its image of criminality to those that have been most associated with specific crime causation theories. They, like Clarke and Cornish, see criminality as a relatively simple and selfish affair—one that has rationality but only of a limited sort.[25] Hirschi and Gottfredson define crimes as events in which force or fraud are used to satisfy self-interest, which for them is simply "the enhancement of pleasure and the avoidance of pain."[26] They assume that if events are to be maximally pleasurable, they should have a certain immediacy, as well as

22. See Ronald V. Clarke and Derek B. Cornish, "Modelling Offender's Decisions: A Framework for Research and Policy," in Michael Tonry and Norval Morris, eds., *Crime and Justice: An Annual Review of Research,* vol. 6, pp. 147–85.

23. Hirschi and Gottfredson, "Causes of White Collar Crime," 971.

24. Hirschi and Gottfredson, "The Significance of White Collar Crime."

25. Derek B. Cornish and Ronald V. Clarke, eds., *The Reasoning Criminal* (New York: Springer Verlag, 1986).

26. Hirschi and Gottfredson, "Causes of White Collar Crime," 959.

a certainty of outcome, and should require minimal effort. With this conception of crime, it follows that "criminality is the tendency of individuals to pursue short-term gratification in the most direct way with little consideration for the long-term consequences of their acts. . . . [P]eople high on this tendency are relatively unable or unwilling to delay gratification; they are relatively indifferent to punishment and to the interests of others. As a consequence, they tend to be impulsive, active, and risk taking."[27]

Whether this view of crime and criminality will turn out to have heuristic value remains to be seen, but it leads Hirschi and Gottfredson to one conclusion that we share, that white-collar occupations tend to require traits like educational persistence, stability of employment, willingness to delay gratification and to work within structures requiring deference to others. From this they infer that the rate of offending among those in white-collar positions ought to be relatively low—probably lower than that associated with other kinds of work.

It would follow from their analysis that, when people commit white-collar crime, they should be operating for the same short-term gratifications and with the same indifference to punishment as the common-crime offender: The securities-fraud offender should have been a youthful mugger but missed the boat. How else do we explain why the average age of a white-collar offender is close to forty, and why most of them are first offenders? In any event, although we admire the ambition to create a general theory of criminality, and recognize that such an ambition is in the spirit of Sutherland, we doubt that it is the wisest path to understanding.

Part of our concern is with the breadth of the concept of crime and criminality itself. As Emile Durkheim noted a century ago, the essential ingredient that all crimes have in common is not their character or origin, but rather their social definition as acts contrary to the laws of the state.[28] Although much criminality is hedonistic, our criminal statutes criminalize acts that could hardly be said to be motivated by immediate and short-term self-interest. In our sample, in addition to tax cheats we have tax protestors, persons who chose to express their

27. Ibid., 959–60.
28. Emile Durkheim, *The Division of Labor in Society,* George Simpson, trans. (New York: Free Press, 1933), see chapter 1.

unhappiness with our government by withholding the monies they owe. They, along with political terrorists or vigilantes, would be hard to explain in the simple terms put forth by a theory of immediate ego gratification.[29]

But suppose we limited our inquiry to the category of "nonviolent crimes engaged in for financial gain." Might we then have an explanation that would be applicable to all such cases? Perhaps at the most general level we would. The one thing the lowliest con man and the highest white-collar offender would seem to share is salesmanship— the capacity to convince others that the person in question is worthy of their trust and their money. The same salesmanship that leads some persons to be chosen as "man of the year" by their companies can also be used for illegitimate purposes. The capacity for concealment or manipulation, for saying things without meaning them, unites virtually all forms of nonviolent, financially motivated frauds. What then differentiates those in the lower reaches of nonviolent offending from those at or near the top of the white-collar crime hierarchy? Even if we agreed with Hirschi and Gottfredson that the proportion of cheats at the higher level ought to be smaller (both for the reasons stated earlier and because being at or near the top does, after all, provide a good living), when it does occur, how do we explain it?

This leads us to the more general question of the motivation underlying white-collar criminal activity. PSIs are not an ideal document for examining motivation, and we would have liked to study the offenders themselves in much more depth than these documents allowed. Yet, our readings of the PSIs identify one trait virtually all of our offenders share (the only major exception being the political tax protestors). The bank teller with children to support, overdue bills, and a husband who took off may not have much else in common with the bank president who is in over his head with investments and real estate deals, but they both share a sense of financial need.

Beyond that common trait, we speculate that there are two rather different paths that may lead to such subjectively felt financial need. On the one hand there are those who have learned early how to use

29. See, for example, David Weisburd, *Jewish Settler Violence: Deviance as Social Reaction* (University Park: The Pennsylvania State University Press, 1989).

salesmanship, guile, and associated techniques to become financially successful. Their effort pays off as they move up the ladder of success. But since the ladder is shaped like a pyramid, competition gets stiffer the further up one goes, and these individuals sooner or later find that they can no longer make the same headway without bending or breaking the rules. They therefore slip over the boundary of legality. These are the high-risk ego gratifiers that Hirschi and Gottfredson identify.

There are others who would be reasonably happy with the place they have achieved through conventional means if only they could keep that place. But the fate of organizational success and failure, or the changing nature of the economy in their line of work, may put them at least temporarily under great financial pressure, where they risk losing the life-style that they have achieved. They may perceive this situation as a short-term threat that can be met through short-term fraud—a temporary taking to be restored as soon as business fortunes turn around. The motivation for their crime is not selfish ego gratification, but rather the fear of falling—of losing what they have worked so hard to gain. It leads them, however, to the same kinds of illegal activity as the former type. But those who follow this path, we speculate, are far more likely to feel the social pain of their conduct when it becomes known and may also feel some genuine remorse for their offenses.

Looked at from afar, these may seem like two very minor variations on the central theme of success and ambition carried to extremes. We believe, however, that when criminality is better understood both general and specific motivations will be seen to play an important part. Our exploration of the problem of white-collar crime leads us to the conclusion that it is unwarranted to assume that each offense requires unique understanding as advocates of specific theories of crime causation have suggested. But our analyses also lead us to the conclusion that going to the other extreme of searching for a single explanation is to ignore the most important lessons that the detailed study of particular kinds of crime can teach us.[30]

30. For an elaboration of these themes, see Stanton Wheeler, "White Collar Crime: Some Reflections on a Socio-Legal Research Program" (paper presented at Edwin Sutherland Conference, Indiana University, May 12–15, 1990).

Policy Implications

It is customary at the close of a major research project to ask if there are policy implications that flow from the investigation or inquiry. It is customary, and also risky. The risk is that most changes in policy, like prescription medicines, have unintended and negative side effects. The arena of white-collar crime is no exception, and as we contemplate changes that might reduce the amount of white-collar criminality or influence the processing of white-collar defendants we recognize that the changes rarely come without cost.

The suggestion that comes closest to the immediate control of the crime itself is to examine organizations closely for where the money is and how it flows. As we noted earlier, with the growth of public and private bureaucracies there are many people, often far from the top of the organizational hierarchy, who have control or sign off power over the flow of money in the organization. Of course, it would take detailed knowledge and familiarity with the particular organization in question to know precisely how to institute controls at the points where the money flows outward, or to decide about the appropriate balance between moral suasion, improved accounting mechanisms, internal or external surveillance, and other mechanisms that might be brought into play to make it harder for those inside to collude with others in efforts to steal from the organization. And for those without an inside connection, organizations may need to improve their capacity to detect the submission of fraudulent documents, reports, or claims.

Organizations have not been blind to these possibilities, and virtually all will have some mechanisms already in place to deal with fraud both from within and from without.[31] But the reading of hundreds of presentence investigations, in which these activities form the backbone of crimes that often continued for months or years without detection, convinces us that many programs really have not put their best organizational intelligence to work on these problems. The persons who commit these offenses are often not the highly sophisticated swindlers portrayed in the mass media, but average people in a financial jam who see a way out through fraud. Develop-

31. Susan P. Shapiro, "The Social Control of Impersonal Trust," *American Journal of Sociology* 93 (1990):623–58.

ment of better mechanisms of detection will also serve a deterrent function and might mean that some of the defendants would be spared the sting and stigma of their criminal activity when they are caught.

These ideas have primarily to do with eliminating the immediate opportunity for crime, or making it abundantly clear that the risks are likely to be far greater than the reward. As we step back from the offense itself toward the motivation of the offender, policy prescriptions become more difficult. Given the enormously important role of credit and debt in the operation of our society, changes in lending and credit rules that would make it harder for people to go into debt would be likely to reduce some of the felt pressure that gets converted into criminal fraud. This is a path that forces delay in gratification and that makes it harder for people to get access to the very material goods that they are encouraged to want by the advertising industry of Madison Avenue. But so long as people are bombarded with messages that encourage spending, it may seem unfair, as well as impractical, to encourage them to contain that spending.

This really takes us back to the basic value structure of our society.[32] If, in the socialization process in the family, neighborhood, and school, persons learn that life's lessons counsel risk taking and the rewards of material affluence rather than honesty and moral integrity, we then can be sure that many will aim for the "fast track," despite running risks of illegality. And here we run right into one of Edwin Sutherland's major themes—namely, that if people are surrounded by definitions of situations favorable to the violation of law they will become law violators. Some imply that this is an arena where it is possible to have your cake and eat it too—to encourage competition, achievement, innovation, the development of new consumer products that make life easier, and simultaneously to reduce the pressures for excessive spending that lead some to the search for a solution through fraud.[33] We disagree. We think it unlikely that a society can maximize both innovation and conformity. Perhaps we

32. Robert Merton reflected on a similar theme some fifty years ago. See Robert K. Merton, "Social Structure and Anomie," *American Sociological Review* 3 (1939):672–82.

33. John Braithwaite, *Crime Shame and Reintegration* (New York: Cambridge University Press, 1989), 158–59. See also Levi, *Regulating Fraud,* chap. 8.

have about the rate of white-collar crime that we "need" in order to encourage the amount of freedom, aspiration, and upward mobility that we seem, as a society, to want.[34]

Our examination of the processing of white-collar defendants in the legal system does not lend itself to simple prescriptions for changes in public policy. But if there is one general conclusion we have reached, it is that those who make decisions about the structuring of the legal process must look beyond the rhetoric surrounding white-collar defendants to the reality of their situations and experiences. In regard to the effects of the legal process on both the lives of defendants and their sentencing by federal judges, we have provided evidence that challenges conventional perceptions and stereotypes.

Should the special impact of the legal process on white-collar defendants be taken into account at time of sentencing? Though we have only partial evidence on this question, our data challenge the premise upon which it is based. Surely, white-collar defendants have farther to fall than most of those convicted of common crimes. Their employment status itself suggests that they have much more to lose as a result of involvement with the legal system. But we were struck by the relative infrequency in which our defendants, their families, or probation officers noted suffering as a result of legal proceedings. This suggests to us that the concern with the special impact of legal involvement may be overstated. At best, it applies to only some white-collar defendants, and often not those highest up the hierarchies of offense and offender.

Our examination of white-collar sentencing suggests that giving judges considerable leeway in arriving at a particular punishment is not inconsistent with calls for greater regularity in sentencing. For the most part, the sentencing practices we identify are consistent with the concerns of those who call for guidelines to constrain judicial behavior.[35] Guidelines have the merit of preventing the most extreme forms of disparity and discrimination. However, there is a

34. In this vein, see Emile Durkheim, *The Rules of Sociological Method,* Sarah A. Solovay and John H. Mueller, trans. (Glencoe: Free Press, 1938). See also Kai T. Erikson, *Wayward Puritans: A Study in the Sociology of Deviance* (New York: John Wiley, 1966).

35. See, for example, Andrew Von Hirsch, Kay A. Knapp, and Michael Tonry, *The Sentencing Commission and Its Guidelines* (Boston: Northeastern University Press, 1987); Schlegel, *Just Deserts.*

degree to which the complex reasoning that judges use in developing sentences cannot be duplicated in the charts and indexes that inform guidelines themselves.[36]

When Edwin H. Sutherland coined the term *white-collar crime,* he sparked interest in an area of study that has often been pursued more in political and rhetorical terms than through sustained empirical research. We have attempted to extend the empirical tradition by examining closely those who have been convicted of white-collar crimes—in terms of both the relation of their backgrounds to the offenses and their subsequent movement through the legal system. In the process, we have been led to a broader conception of white-collar crime than that which informed and animated Sutherland's pathbreaking work. It is a conception that includes the corporate offenders that most concerned Sutherland, to be sure, but one that puts greater emphasis on the opportunities available to middle-class Americans, whether in organizations or not.

Our concept takes cognizance of the vast middle of American society and its susceptibility to financial wrongdoing. This category tended to be neglected by Sutherland, who concentrated on the apex of white-collar offending, and by those who have emphasized the street crimes of an urban underclass. As the nation approaches the twenty-first century, we anticipate that the kinds of nonviolent economic crimes examined in this book will grow in significance. For these are the crimes that modern bureaucracies bring within the reach of virtually every American citizen.

36. The extent to which judges are now allowed to depart from the strict standards of the federal guidelines system attests to this fact (United States Sentencing Commission, *Sentencing Guidelines and Policy Statements* [Washington, D.C.: GPO, 1987], chap. 5, part K).

Appendix 1:
The Makeup of the Sample

Table A–1 Number of Individuals in the Basic Sample, by Offense and District

				District				
Offense	Southern New York	Maryland	Northern Georgia	Northern Texas	Northern Illinois	Central California	Western Washington	Total
Bank Embezzlement	30	29	22	30	30	30	30	201
Tax Fraud	30	30	30	30	30	30	30	210
Credit Fraud	30	6	22	30	16	30	24	158
Mail Fraud	30	30	30	30	30	30	10	190
Securities Fraud	30	0	0	5	1	30	1	67
False Claims	30	8	25	24	14	30	26	157
Bribery	30	11	0	8	16	17	2	84
Antitrust	15	4	6	0	0	2	0	27
All White-Collar Crimes	225	118	135	157	137	199	123	1,094
Common Crimes	30	30	30	30	30	30	30	210

Note: The sampling design is discussed in chapter 1. Unless otherwise noted, the sample of white-collar criminals here is used whenever we discuss white-collar criminals as a group. This sample of common criminals is used throughout.

Table A–2   Supplemental Securities and Antitrust Offenders, by
Offense and District

	District			
Offense	Southern New York	Central California	Other	Total
Securities Fraud	57	2	99	158
Antitrust	0	0	90	90
Total	57	2	189	248

Note: This sample is combined with the basic sample in the descriptions of
securities and antitrust offenders in chapters 3 and 5. This sample includes
individuals convicted of securities and antitrust outside of the seven basic
districts. It also includes those convicted of securities violations within the
seven districts who were not included in the basic sample because there were
more than 30 individuals convicted of securities violations within those specific districts (see chapter 1).

Table A–3 Supplemental Codefendants, by Offense and District

	District							
Offense	Southern New York	Maryland	Northern Georgia	Northern Texas	Northern Illinois	Central California	Western Washington	Total
Bank Embezzlement	8	0	0	4	1	11	0	24
Tax Fraud	5	4	2	0	0	6	2	19
Credit Fraud	2	0	0	0	0	6	0	8
Mail Fraud	29	6	17	17	23	19	0	111
False Claims	20	0	0	0	0	10	0	30
Bribery	12	0	0	0	0	0	0	12
Total	76	10	19	21	24	52	2	204

Note: These are those codefendants of individuals in the basic sample who are not themselves in either the basic sample or the supplemental securities and antitrust sample. They are used to describe the characteristics of cases in chapters 2 and 5.

Appendix 2:
The Relationship between the Number of Individual Offenders and the Number of Cases, by Offense and District

Cases (Individuals)[1]

District

Offense	Southern New York	Maryland	Northern Georgia	Northern Texas	Northern Illinois	Central California	Western Washington	Other	Total
Bank Embezzlement	25 (30)	28 (29)	22 (22)	29 (30)	28 (30)	25 (30)	30 (30)	0 (0)	187 (201)
Tax Fraud	27 (30)	28 (30)	28 (30)	30 (30)	30 (30)	27 (30)	29 (30)	0 (0)	199 (210)
Credit Fraud	27 (30)	6 (6)	16 (22)	29 (30)	14 (16)	24 (30)	23 (24)	0 (0)	139 (158)
Mail Fraud	19 (30)	27 (30)	19 (30)	19 (30)	20 (30)	22 (30)	8 (10)	0 (0)	134 (190)
Securities Fraud	44[2] (87)	0 (0)	0 (0)	4 (5)	1 (1)	15 (30)	1 (1)	50 (99)	115 (225)
False Claims	23 (30)	8 (8)	20 (25)	20 (24)	14 (14)	28 (30)	24 (26)	0 (0)	137 (157)
Bribery	18 (30)	5 (11)	0 (0)	7 (8)	15 (16)	14 (17)	2 (2)	0 (0)	61 (84)
Antitrust	3 (15)	2 (4)	1 (6)	0 (0)	0 (0)	1 (2)	0 (0)	31 (90)	38 (117)
All White-Collar Crimes	186 (282)	104 (118)	106 (135)	138 (157)	122 (137)	156 (201)	117 (123)	81 (189)	1,010 (1,342)
Common Crimes	30 (30)	28 (30)	29 (30)	30 (30)	29 (30)	30 (30)	28 (30)	0 (0)	204 (210)

[1]The number of individuals from these cases in the basic sample or the national samples of securities and antitrust offenders
[2]Includes 14 cases represented by at least 1 person in the basic sample and 30 cases not represented in the basic sample in Appendix 1.

Appendix 3:
The Most Common Statutes
and Corresponding Penalties

Title: Section	Description	Maximum fine	Maximum prison sentence
15:1	Sherman Antitrust Act		
	—individual	$100,000	1 year
	—corporation	$500,000	—
15:77	Securities Act of 1933		
	—domestic	$10,000	5 years
	Securities subchapter (penalty provision is 15:77ff.)		
15:78	Securities Exchange Act of 1934 (penalty provision is 15:78ff.)	$10,000	5 years
18:201	Bribery of public official (18:201b–e)	$20,000 or 3 times bribe	15 years
	Bribery in official act (18:201f–i)	$10,000	2 years
18:287	False, fictitious, or fraudulent claims	$10,000	5 years
18:371	Conspiracy (unless misdemeanor, then maximum = maximum of misdemeanor)	$10,000	5 years
18:495	Forgery (false, altered, or forged deed, contract, etc.)	$1,000	10 years

Title: Section	Description	Maximum fine	Maximum prison sentence
18:656	Theft, embezzlement, or misappli-cation by bank officer or em-ployee, if $100	$5,000 $1,000	5 years 1 year
18:1001	False, fictitious, or fraudulent statements or entries	$10,000	5 years
18:1005	False bank entries	$5,000	5 years
18:1006	False credit institution entries	$10,000	5 years
18:1010	False claim to HUD or FHA for loans	$5,000	2 years
18:1012	False statement to HUD	$1,000	1 year
18:1014	False statement in loan or credit application	$5,000	2 years
18:1341	Mail frauds and swindles	$1,000	5 years
18:1343	Fraud by wire, radio, or television	$1,000	5 years
18:1701	Obstruction of mails	$100	6 mos.
18:1708	Theft or receipt of stolen mail	$2,000	5 years
26:7201	Attempt to evade or defeat tax	$10,000	5 years
26:7203	Failure to file return, supply infor-mation, or pay tax	$10,000	1 year
26:7205	Fraudulent withholding state-ment	$500	1 year
26:7206	False or fraudulent statement	$5,000	3 years
26:7207	Fraudulent returns, statements, or other documents	$1,000	1 year

Index

(Italics indicate information in table/figure.)